THE AIRPLANE GRAVEYARD

The Forgotten WWII Warbirds of Kwajalein Atoll

BRANDI MUELLER   ALAN AXELROD

A PERMUTED PRESS BOOK
ISBN: 978-1-68261-771-7

The Airplane Graveyard:
The Forgotten WWII Warbirds of Kwajalein Atoll
© 2018 by Brandi Mueller
All Rights Reserved

Cover design by Cody Corcoran
Interior design by Diana Lawrence

Permuted Press, LLC
New York • Nashville
permutedpress.com

Published in the United States of America
Printed in China

Dedicated to the crews who flew these warbirds

We brought an American flag down to the Airplane Graveyard to celebrate Memorial Day several years ago.

TABLE OF CONTENTS

Some of the small islands and islets that make up Kwajalein Atoll

INTRODUCTION: KWAJ

Maps depict the Pacific Ocean as a vast expanse of blue with a few dots of green, which make it look as if this grand ocean is almost nothing but water. In reality, within those watery miles are countless islands. A few names—Hawaii, Tahiti, Fiji—instantly conjure scenes of pearly white sand, palm trees, and magenta sunsets. But there are so many other islands, including bits of land it seems no one had heard of before World War II, and very few have thought of since.

It was these obscure little islands, mostly, that played the biggest roles in the war's Pacific Theater. Yet, as anonymously as they emerged into popular consciousness, so they have receded from it, at least for people living on the continents.

One such group of "forgotten" islands are the ninety-seven of Kwajalein Atoll, today part of the Republic of the Marshall Islands. Most of the 13,500 Marshall Islanders who live on the atoll make their homes on Ebeye Island, but eleven islands are leased by the U.S. military as part of the Ronald Reagan Ballistic Missile Defense Test Site. U.S. military personnel and other English-speaking residents call the atoll Kwaj, as do the few visitors who are attracted by a tropical paradise, whose waters vary in shades of perfect blue and whose emerald palm trees sway ever so slightly in the breeze.

Tropical paradise

Kwaj is just one of the twenty-nine atolls and five individual islands within 750,000 square miles of ocean that make up the Republic of the Marshall Islands (RMI). Altogether, this is about seventy square miles of land. If 750,000 square miles of ocean is an area the size of Mexico, the land, altogether, is the city of Seattle split into twenty-nine thin sections and scattered across a liquid Mexico. Divide those slivers into fifteen to thirty tiny islands each. That is the RMI, a nation of 53,158 people and 1,156 individual islands and islets.

Kwaj rests almost in the middle of the Pacific, 2,400 miles southwest of Hawaii, 2,000 miles from Australia, and 500 miles north of the Equator. It is a collection of coral reef islands created from a barrier reef, which at one time in geological history encircled a volcanic island. The volcanic island long ago eroded back into the ocean, leaving a ring of tiny islands around a large body of water—the lagoon. The island called Kwajalein, largest in the atoll, is just 1.2 square miles: 1.2 miles long by 800 yards wide. Like all of the Marshall Islands, it has a very low elevation, the highest point in the country being just shy of forty-six feet in an average elevation of six feet above sea level.

Left: Night sky from Roi

Below: Beautiful above and below

9

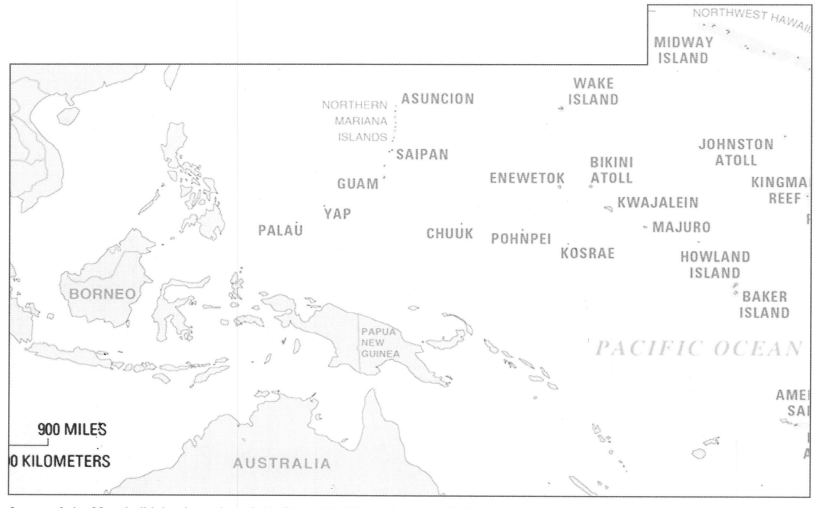

A map of the Marshall Islands region of the South Pacific, with Australia lower left, the Hawaiian Islands upper right, and Kwajalein at center, right (map courtesy USGS)

The Marshalls were settled by Micronesians sometime in the second millennium BC and were "discovered" by Alonso de Salazar of Spain in 1526. After an English explorer, John Marshall, visited in 1788, the islands were named for him (No one asked the islanders about it!). Spain claimed the Marshalls in 1874, and Germany bought them from Spain eleven years later for $4.5 million. With the outbreak of World War I, Japan—which had joined the Allies opposing Germany—took control of the Marshalls. Twenty years later, early in World War II, the Japanese military, now Germany's ally, occupied Kwajalein Atoll, which the U.S. military assaulted on January 31, 1944, defeating the Japanese occupiers on February 3.

That Battle of Kwajalein was the tenth major battle out of the twenty-three the United States fought in the Pacific Theater of World War II. It was in the Pacific that the war had begun for the United States on December 7, 1941, when Japanese aircraft carriers launched a devastating surprise attack on U.S. Army and Navy bases at Pearl Harbor, Hawaii Territory. Although U.S. Army Air Corps lieutenant colonel (later general) James H. "Jimmy" Doolittle led a small but daring reprisal air raid on Tokyo and other mainland Japanese targets on April 18, 1942, which greatly lifted American morale, the news from the Pacific Theater was dire for America and its allies for roughly the first seven months of combat. Japan invaded the Philippines and Guam,

Left: The Air Operations Command Building.

Below: Bunker on Roi-Namur

both American possessions, on December 10. They invaded Burma, British Borneo, and Hong Kong, all parts of the American-allied British Empire, between the 11th and the 18th. Wake Island, which had a U.S. Navy and Marine base, fell to the Japanese on December 23, 1941. British-held Singapore was besieged on January 30, 1942. By April 1942, all these places were in Japanese hands, in addition to Java, Sumatra, and the Dutch East Indies. As for the Pacific Islands, New Britain, Bougainville, Bali, Tulagi, and others were occupied by the Japanese military.

Japan's war-winning strategy was to advance outward from its home islands, taking territory that provided the nation with much-needed raw materials for both national survival and war-making while also creating a series of vast defensive rings far out into the Pacific. During May 4-8, 1942, despite having been badly battered at Pearl Harbor, the U.S. Pacific Fleet engaged the Japanese Imperial Navy in the Battle of the Coral Sea. Although the Japanese sank more ships than the Americans did, thus winning a tactical victory, the U.S. Navy achieved a strategic triumph by arresting the Japanese Pacific advance, which so far had been unstoppable.

The Battle of the Coral Sea was followed by the Battle of Midway (June 4-7, 1942), a costly but decisive American victory, which inflicted losses on the Japanese fleet from which the Imperial Navy never recovered. After Midway, Japan went into a long defensive retreat in the Pacific Theater while U.S. forces pressed the offensive. Each battle from Midway on was an American victory—often very costly, but each advanced U.S. forces closer to Japan itself. After Midway came the hard-fought victory in the bitterly long Guadalcanal Campaign (August 7, 1942-February 9, 1943) and the Gilbert and Marshall Islands Campaign, which began with the Makin Island Raid (August 17-18, 1942). The vicious Battle of Tarawa came next, on November 20, 1943, along with the Battle of Makin, spanning November 20-23.

The Battle of Kwajalein was fought from January 31 to February 3, 1944. It was the principal action of Operation Flintlock, the culminating phase of a U.S. offensive in the Marshalls that spanned January 31 to February 21, 1944 and included invasions of three of the Marshall atolls—Majuro, Kwajalein, and Eniwetok. The operation is discussed in chapter three, and while it was yet another American victory, the war for the Pacific islands would not end until twelve more major battles had been won, the last two of which were the bloodiest, at Iwo Jima (February 19, 1945) and Okinawa (April 1, 1945). Even then, the Pacific war ground on until the atomic bombings of Hiroshima and Nagasaki on August 6 and 9, 1945.

It is very difficult to picture today the brutal ferocity of what took place on Kwaj not so very long ago. But the white sands that blush pink in an equatorial sunset were once soaked deeply with the blood of intensely determined combatants. At first sight, Kwajalein Atoll reveals no tokens of its violent past. But look just a little closer, and you can find the remains of Japanese buildings overgrown by tropical jungle. If you are a diver, like me and others who visit Kwaj, there are far more dramatic reminders of a very different time waiting to be discovered in the waters below the glowing sunset.

Inset: American soldiers dig in at Iwo Jima (Public Domain)
Below: The battleship USS Idaho unleashes on Okinawa (Public Domain)

Above: The mushroom cloud after the atomic bomb
is dropped on Nagasaki (Public Domain)

Right: Japanese casement on the beach of Roi-
Namur

Above: Japanese building, possibly a warehouse, on Roi-Namur
Right: With views like this, it's hard to picture the brutality that occurred here.

Kwajalein Atoll has one of the largest ocean lagoons on earth. Within these 324 square- miles is an undersea museum of Pacific Theater strife. It is a graveyard of sorts. While the remains of flesh, blood, and bone have long ago mingled their atoms with the ocean's elements, the steel, iron, and aluminum of sunken Japanese warships, crashed airplanes, artillery, and ammunition rest on the lagoon floor. One area, two miles square, is filled with American warbirds, not shot down, but rudely discarded beneath the sapphire water, symbols of America's rush to demobilize after the atomic bombs

brought the seemingly endless World War II to a sudden end. Costly weapons such as fighter planes were now considered just so much bulky, heavy junk: war surplus too expensive to transport 4,000 miles back to the United States for inevitable disposal as scrap. Troops clamored to go home and, at home, their families clamored to have them back. Space on ships had to be cleared for heroes with civilian futures ahead of them. There was no room for hardware already bound for obsolescence and unlikely to be needed again any time soon.

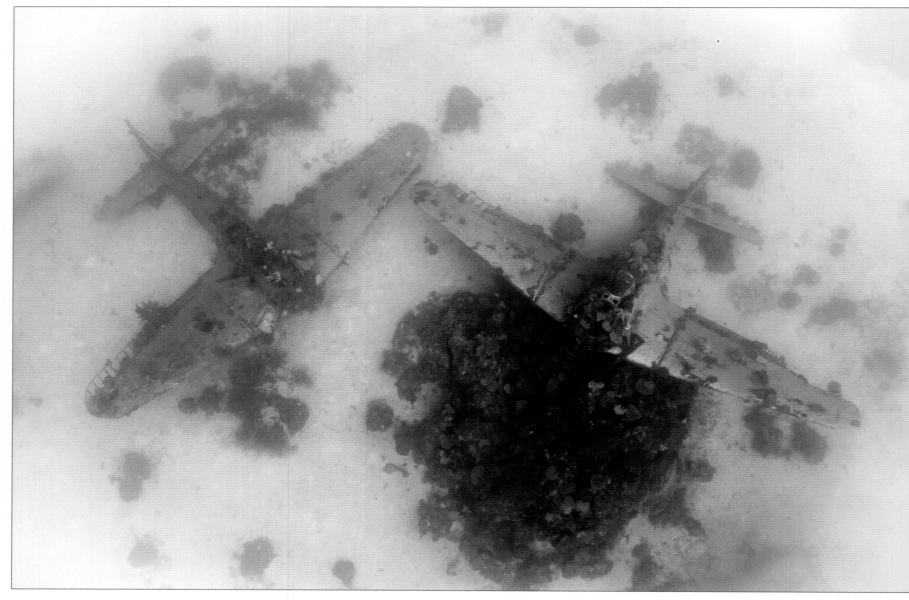

Two Douglas Dauntless warbirds discarded after the war

Japan signed an "instrument of surrender" aboard the battleship Missouri riding at anchor in Tokyo Bay on September 2, 1945. In October, an estimated 150 American aircraft were unceremoniously stripped of whatever salvageable parts were likely to remain useful, loaded aboard a barge, towed out to the north end of the Kwaj lagoon—which averages 100 to 130 feet deep—pushed off the barge deck, and consigned to oblivion.

Or not.

Scuba divers visit an upside down TBF Avenger

In some areas you can see more than six or seven planes in one area.

Right: A diver visits a PBJ-1 Mitchell.

A PBJ being prepared to be dumped off Roi-Namur in October, 1945 (Photo by Staff Sergeant Farley R. Lund, courtesy Bill Remick collection)

Dumped at the north end of the lagoon, the aircraft were unwittingly preserved in water deep enough to protect them from storms and other hazards over the years, but still shallow enough for scuba divers, like me, to visit and photograph them. Had they been dumped on the ocean side of the atoll, they would indeed have found oblivion. There the drop-off quickly plunges thousands of feet, reachable, if at all, only by cutting-edge submersibles. At Kwaj, divers can explore an underwater gallery of largely intact World War II American warbirds. There are seven major types there: the Douglas SBD Dauntless, Vought F4U Corsair, Curtiss SB2C Helldiver, Curtiss C-46 Commando, Grumman F4F Wildcat, Grumman TBF Avenger, and the PBJ-1 Mitchell, which is the Navy and Marine Corps version of the U.S. Army Air Force's twin-engine B-25 medium bomber. On April 18, 1942, sixteen of these iconic "Mitchell" bombers flew from the deck of the carrier *Hornet* in the famed "Doolittle Raid" against Tokyo and other Japanese targets in America's first offensive blow against the enemy.

The planes are now home to marine life such as these Moorish idols that swim along the cockpit

diver examines a spare propeller stuffed into the cockpit of the Vought F4U Corsair.

A green sea turtle on a reef

CHAPTER 1
DIVER

grew up in northern Wisconsin, an unlikely place to develop an interest in World War II aviation wreck-diving and an even less likely locale for anyone to develop an obsession with the ocean. Lucky for me, I spent many weeks of my childhood winters visiting family in Florida and Hawaii, and, after I saw my first manatee when I was seven, my destiny was set. Instantly, I was the little girl, bundled up in thirty-below winters, who told my teachers how I was going to be a marine biologist when I grew up.

My itch to explore the world started early. I successfully begged my parents to let me be a foreign exchange

A scuba diver observes Douglas Dauntless warbirds discarded after the war.

Being underwater, breathing underwater, changes your life

student to New Zealand when I was fifteen. Friends of my host family were divers, and I eagerly seized the opportunity to take scuba lessons with the objective of getting certified as an Open Water diver. First, though, I had to call home— an extravagance in those mostly pre-cellular days—to persuade my parents to fund this "once in a lifetime opportunity," which, I argued, was cheap at $180. (And it was!).

They wired the money to my New Zealand bank account, and, in company with another exchange student, I became a diver. We remain best friends to this day. The ocean and diving—they create powerful bonds.

I didn't dive again until college, when I studied biology at the University of Tampa. My focus was mostly on marine biology, but I was earnestly trying to remain open-minded to other fields of biology as well. I worked part-time at a marina for a man who was the sea salt of the Caribbean, having lived and worked on the islands for most of his life, including in Monserrat and Little Cayman. He had been a diver since, well, essentially the dawn of scuba, and I loved nothing more than spending rum thirties with him (and anyone else who happened by that day) in his office at the end of a workday, talking about diving in the Caribbean before there were dive shops...or, for that matter, much of a concern for safety.

He returned to his beloved Little Cayman several times a year, where he had owned a dive resort. Knowing that I was a certified diver, he invited me on a trip with his friends and family. I worked extra shifts at the marina and after another one of those phone calls home, my infinitely supportive parents loaned me the rest of the money I needed to go on a week-long dive trip to Little Cayman. The trip was incredible. Not the least of its gifts was my realization that I was a terrible diver who had a lot to learn. But I was eager to learn it all because that trip made me remember how fascinating it was to be underwater, and it made me want to become more skilled and spend more time below. Little Cayman has some of the most beautiful wall diving in the world. Sheer underwater cliffs are covered in vibrant sponges and corals—a forest that is home to an infinite array of colorful fish zipping and zooming around the reef. Sharks, turtles, and eagle rays pass you. On each dive, when my tank started to run low, my only desire was to stay down longer.

As soon as I got back to Tampa I signed up for an Advanced Open Water class, which was taught on campus

Colorful sponges underwater off Little Cayman

and even gave my GPA a boost. The next semester I took Rescue Diver training and the semester after that, Divemaster certification. I was hooked. The dive shop that offered classes on campus let me continue to dive with them when they were teaching other classes so I could get more DM experience. I graduated with a biology degree, a chemistry minor, and I qualified as a PADI Divemaster. My plan now was to take a year or two off to travel before returning for grad school. After reading an article in *Sport Diver* magazine by its "teen editor" about a summer camp-like program that taught her to dive and sail in the Caribbean, I became instantly jealous. I called my mother to ask why she and dad hadn't thought to send me to such a program in-between my jaunt to New Zealand and the dozens of extra-curriculars I took part in. She wasn't especially receptive to hearing me complain about "her" oversight, so I found the program online and sent an email: "Hi, I'm so sad I didn't get to do this as a teenager, do you have any job openings?"

They hired me, and four weeks later I was in Key Largo completing my PADI Open Water Scuba Instructor course.

Kona is known for its Manta Ray Night dive, where you can see dozen of mantas coming in to feed on the plankton that is attracted to divers' lights

Spinner dolphins off the coast of Kona, Hawaii

Two days after passing the instructor exam, I was on a plane to the British Virgin Islands. I spent that summer living aboard a forty-foot sailboat with a dozen teenagers for three weeks at a time. I taught them how to dive. I taught them how to sail. And I even taught them some marine biology. As for the sailing, I learned as I taught.

In the blink of an eye, a summer of sheer character-building alongside a staff of some of the most amazing people I had ever met was over. I was back on a plane with a paycheck for some of the most intense work I'd ever done. It was hardly enough for a cup of coffee. I was exhausted and impoverished, but my life was changed. I loved boats. I loved eating, sleeping, and just being on the ocean. There was nothing better than waking up every morning to the sunrise on the water and then sleeping under a million stars as gentle waves rocked me to sleep in a hammock (Did I mention I slept in a hammock all summer?). And, of course, going scuba diving all the time. Maybe it would have been even better without a dozen sixteen-year-olds. But to do what you want, you do what you must.

I started to look for full-time diving and boat jobs but was still dedicated to my year of travel, so I went to South America. A month later, somewhere in Peru, I got an email from the *Kona Aggressor*, a liveaboard scuba diving boat that did week-long dive trips along the Kona coast. If I could be in Hawaii in one week, I had a job. I replied to the email, packed my bag, and spent the next year of my life on a luxury liveaboard, leading dives on the southwest coast of the Big Island of Hawaii. I also made beds, cleaned toilets, and washed more dishes than I had ever washed in my life. Once again, however, I made lifelong friends with several of my crewmates and even a few of the guests who came aboard.

I had not lost sight of a mental deadline for graduate school, and I applied while I was on the boat. In the spring I got an interview at the University of Hawaii. On a Saturday, the day our previous week's guests got off the boat and new guests got on in the afternoon, the captain allowed me to fly to Oahu for my interview, provided I flew back that night in time for the charter to start.

Just a few weeks short of a year on the *Kona Aggressor*, I moved to Oahu to start graduate school. My first night living on Oahu was spent sitting on the floor, crying.

What *had* I done?

I quit the best job I ever had. I left people who had been the best and worst dysfunctional family I ever had (Living and working with five other people on a 100-foot vessel is automatically a soap opera). We loved each other, hated each other, dated each other, and broke up with each other. Some days we wouldn't speak to each other, but still smiled and acted like we were best friends while interacting with the fourteen guests on board. It was amazing and terrible at the same time, and no matter how bad the social part of the job sometimes got, my main job was to go diving every day. What was I thinking of, leaving this?

Grad school started. Hawaii was expensive. So, I started looking for dive jobs on Oahu. The same online diver classifieds in which I had found the *Kona Aggressor* had a listing for Dive Oahu. The response to my email was immediate. I had an interview—at six the very next morning. Under other circumstances, this would have seemed ridiculous even to me. But I was living on the North Shore and commuting to Honolulu every day in rush hour traffic that was out of a horror movie. Most mornings, I was out the door at four just to beat the traffic. Six in the a.m.? Piece of cake.

I met with the manager since the owner was running late. He hired me before the owner even showed up, and they wanted me to start right away, as in at *eight*—that morning. For the next five years, I worked on the dive boat as a dive guide and eventually as a captain, a dive instructor, at the retail shops throughout the island, and as the company's first-ever travel coordinator. I took groups for weekend trips to the other islands, and I also led trips to Fiji and Palau.

Yes, I found time to complete my master's degree, and I even dug into a PhD. After two years of that it dawned on me that I enjoyed being on the water more than looking at the water from an office window. I left Oahu, first to go back to the *Kona Aggressor* as a mate and photography pro, and then to other boats in the fleet in Turks and Caicos, the Dominican Republic, and Papua New Guinea.

While I had been living on Oahu, two fellow members of the Kona Aggressor crew moved to an island in the middle of the Pacific Ocean so small that I couldn't find it on any map. At the time, I thought they were nuts: "You're moving *where*?" It was one of a small group of tiny islands that hosted the US Army base that was part of the Ronald Reagan Ballistic Missile Defense Test Site. My friends were civilian employees in the Army's Marine Department, working

The first WWII airplane I ever saw – a Corsair off Oahu that was ditched in 1948 after running out of fuel and the pilot survived

on boats by day while spending their nights and weekends scuba diving in what sounded like some of the best diving on the planet.

There was no way I wasn't going to visit. Although it wasn't as simple as buying a plane ticket and showing up at the airport. My friend Amber had to submit an official request for me to visit, but only after I had provided the United States government with enough personal details for someone to steal a lifetime supply of my identity. After several weeks of anxious waiting, I was approved.

That was exactly half the battle. Actually getting to Kwajalein was the other half. The Island Hopper—formerly Continental Micronesia and now operated by United—departs

Honolulu three times a week. After seven hours of flying and a quick stop in Majuro, capital city (population 27,797) of the Marshall Islands, the flight embarks for the island of Kwajalein, largest island of Kwajalein Atoll.

Bleary-eyed, I opened the window shade upon the same endless blue that had been my view for seven hours. As the pilot came over the PA to admonish us that taking photographs out the window was forbidden because Kwajalein is a "secure US Military installation," an oval of yellow and green surrounded by a ring of breaking white waves slipped into view.

The atoll is shaped vaguely like a boomerang, and people living on the island tell you that's because once you reach it, you keep coming back. On board the plane, we were informed that passengers cannot deplane unless they are staying on Kwajalein (with military orders) or going via the ferry to Ebeye, most populous island in the atoll. As I got off the plane, the remaining passengers were only other Pacific Islanders, a missionary or two, and some scuba divers headed to Chuuk to dive the WWII wrecks there. The Island Hopper dropped me off on Kwaj and continued to Kosrae, Pohnpei, Chuuk, and, finally, to Guam. The next day it would start the same circuit back to Honolulu. No flights on Sundays.

Kwajalein has only about 1,200 residents, mostly military contractors, a few active duty personnel, their families, and some Marshallese who work and live on base. Most Marshall Islanders are not permitted to live on Kwajalein. They make their homes five miles north on Ebeye, which is today one of the most densely populated strips of land on earth.

Once off the plane, we were escorted to a security holding area, where we were briefed on what we could and could not do on Kwajalein. I was then photographed and given a badge with my photo.

Ebeye Island from the airplane window

One of the many beaches on Kwaj

A surfer's board seen from underwater off Kwajalein

"Carry it at *all times*," I was warned. The badge listed who I was as well as who was sponsoring me. Amber, my sponsor, was totally on the hook for my behavior. She was waiting for me on the other side of the fence, and I was immediately enamored with this little island, where you rode a bike everywhere and enjoyed cold beers watching the sunset on empty beaches. And this was even before she took me diving.

She took me on some of my first wreck dives. I had already done some wreck diving, but mostly "exploring" deliberately sunk ships—vessels that had been cleaned up and scuttled on purpose for the use of divers and to help

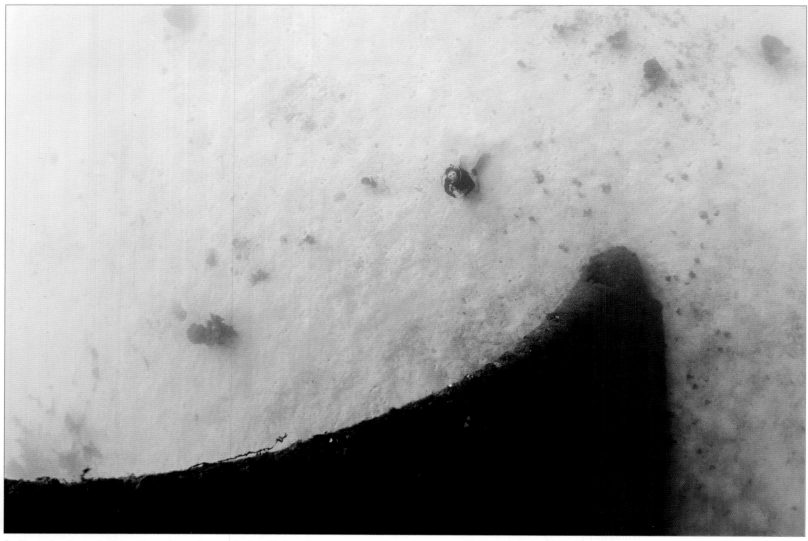

A diver is dwarfed by the giant bow of the *Prinz Eugen*, one of the best shipwreck dives Kwajalein has to offer

encourage marine life growth. The ships in Kwaj were World War II-vintage Japanese vessels that had been sent to the bottom in combat. They had massive guns on their bows and ammunition in their lockers—quite possibly still live. They were also covered in the stunning marine life found only in the world's healthiest ocean environments. Red sea fans, purple soft corals. Nurse sharks slept on decks and turtles rested on masts. Fish? Fish were everywhere.

The reef diving was also spectacular. The shipwrecks in the lagoon were shallow, at least compared to the ocean side of the atoll, with its abysmal drop of some several thousand feet. Oceanside dives had crystal clear water, hard coral fields swarming with fish, and lots of big animals like sharks, dolphins, mantas, and eagle rays passing by divers in the blue.

Amber also took me to Roi-Namur, another Army-leased island, this one at the northeast corner of the atoll. To get there, you catch a ride on the "metro," the name for small fixed-wing aircraft that make the forty-mile run several times a day on weekdays and twice on weekends. For Kwaj residents, visiting Roi can be a mini vacation. The island is mostly overgrown with dense jungle. Fewer than 100 full-time residents live on it, and there's a great little bar

Amber giant-steps off the boat at the beginning of a dive

Sharks at a dive site known as Troy's Coral Head

Left: A lionfish, with a wreck known as Barracuda Junction
or Choko Maru behind

Above: A diver visits the Palawan wreck

and restaurant called the Outrigger, which has the best burgers west of the International Date Line.

Roi-Namur used to be two separate islands, but, during the Japanese occupation either before or during World War II, conscripted Korean laborers built a causeway between the two, and it has been officially Roi-Namur ever since, though everyone persists in calling it Roi. Randomly distributed around the quiet island are benches facing the ocean.

You can sit, contemplate the water, and usually see no one else for hours. The island has several beach shacks, maintained by residents and furnished with hammocks, beach chairs, some even with a refrigerator to keep the beer cold.

Anemone fish on the reef

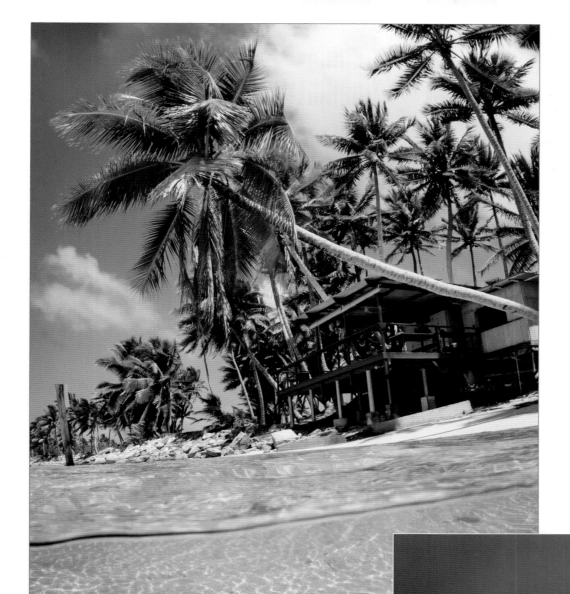

The Gabby Shack on Roi-Namur, one of my favorite places on the island

White tip shark on the reef

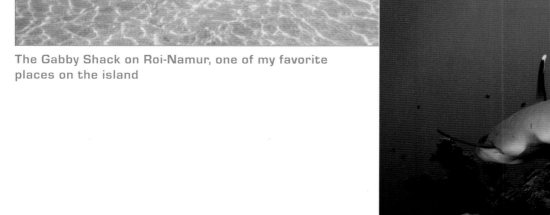

Japanese Gun emplacement on Roi-Namur

Inside one of the Japanese building ruins,
largely intact after more than 75 years

The remains of quite a few Japanese military buildings dot the landscape, including a mostly intact command structure, bunkers, ammo dumps, and, largely reclaimed by the jungle, a hospital, a water collection building, a storage building, and others. In many places, the poured concrete used to make the walls has worn away, exposing rusted skeletal rebar.

It goes without saying that the diving is fantastic. Three Japanese shipwrecks are just off shore, as well as a Mitsubishi A6M "Zeke," better known as a Zero, icon of the Imperial Japanese Navy's air arm. The coral reefs are gorgeous. But my personal favorite destination is the Airplane Graveyard.

I still remember my first dive on it. We were only on Roi for one night before returning to Kwaj and had time for only one dive. Amber took me to the site everyone calls the "Airplane Graveyard," or "13 Planes" because you usually can see thirteen SBDs (Douglas SBD Dauntless aircraft). I descended on the site, and my first glimpse of planes were two SBDs resting upright on the edge of a large coral mound. Continuing past those, I saw two more SBDs, nose down and without wings, and two upright planes, the sand almost touching the nose of each. From there you can pick any direction and see SBDs in the distance. If you move fast you can see all thirteen in one dive. We saw probably ten

The Corsair in the Airplane Graveyard

A site in the Airplane Graveyard called "13 Planes" was the first dive I did on the graveyard. As many as thirteen planes can be seen in one dive.

that day. I was amazed. At the time, I didn't know there were some 140 more aircraft in the area.

I visited Kwajalein two more times, and when I returned for the fourth, it was to stay. I got a job as a civilian contractor captaining ferry boats. People back home thought I was crazy. What do you expect when you tell them you are moving to a tiny island in the middle of the Pacific to work as a ferry captain?

It didn't bother me. I was excited. I packed up all my belongings, which wasn't much beyond dive gear, camera gear, a new bike for my Kwaj vehicular transport, and a paddleboard—which just seemed like something I'd want there. I took the Island Hopper out of Honolulu. On arrival this time, I was given a badge with my photo, the name of the company I worked for, and what areas of the atoll I was allowed to visit. It was also my electronic meal card for three meals a day at the Army mess hall.

My new home was a studio apartment in the BQs (Bachelor Quarters) with its own bathroom and kitchenette. The island had a small grocery store, convenience store (think 7-Eleven), and a few other small shops where you could find lots of stuff—provided it wasn't something you actually needed. There was a Burger King, a Subway, and pizza place. Impressive, if you don't mind that they were usually out of whatever you most wanted, such as lettuce or turkey meat. Even if they did happen to have on hand what you most coveted, it was always slightly different from what you expected. Even so, these places were a break in the mess hall monotony.

To keep us entertained there were two outdoor movie theaters, a bowling alley, a golf course (nine holes on Kwaj, nine on Roi), a fitness center, a suite of sports complexes (basketball, tennis, racquetball, volley ball), two pools, and two bars: the Snake Pit and the Vet's Hall—or three if you count the Country Club, which was open only occasionally for special events. People were actually hired to run "Community Activities," which scheduled the likes of intramural volleyball and other sports, bar events like karaoke, and other forms of island entertainment.

For the scuba divers there was the Kwajalein Scuba Club. A cheap membership fee gave you unlimited use of scuba tanks for the year. You could dive right off the beach, and on weekends there was a small harbor that rented boats, allowing us to move farther out to dive on the WWII wrecks. Still, some people never adjusted to island life, which is, in a word, isolated. We were really, really far away from everything familiar. There were no cell phones, not much shopping, and no "nice" sit-down restaurants. There was internet, but it was painfully slow. Phone calls to anyplace off-island were crackly, and snail mail from the states took forever to arrive (On the other hand, who can complain that stuff ordered off

Amazon took a few weeks? You were getting whatever you wanted in the *middle of nowhere*!). Some folks knew right away that the Kwaj life was not for them. We all heard stories of people who got off the plane, took one look, and got right back on. Others gave no notice, packed their things, bought a plane ticket out, and were never seen again. Me? I loved it (mostly).

In fact, it is easy to get involved in the community and become surprisingly busy on a tiny island. There were bingo and trivia nights, you could play or just attend intramural sports matches, and there was scuba. My work hours were either 4 a.m. to 1 p.m., or 1 p.m. to 9 p.m., which gave me the ability to either dive in the morning or, after getting off work at one, ride my bike to the tank house, grab a few tanks, and be underwater by two. Not a bad life.

My job was pretty great as well. I mean, who doesn't want to captain a ferry boat? I had up to 150 passengers per trip between Kwaj and Ebeye. On any given day I spent either sunrise or sunset driving a boat, and on some

Left: A diver descends down the kingpost of a WWII Japanese wreck into a mass of fish.

Below: A colorful anemone fish on the reef in a bright purple anemone

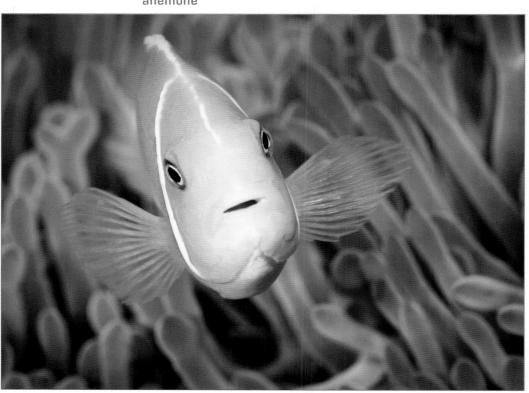

Left: The reefs provide nonstop entertainment for divers from turtles, to sharks, to wrecks

Ready to dive

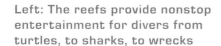

One of the ferry boat's I captained

At work

days, doing double shifts, I saw both the sunrise and the sunset. The view out of *this* office window was invariably spectacular.

During my last eighteen months working on the atoll, I drove the ferry boat on Roi, in the same way local workers lived on Ebeye and came to work on Kwajalein, at the north end of the atoll, the local workforce lived on Ennibur (also called Third Island) and came over to work on Roi. I

would spend a week at a time up there, which gave me much more opportunity to dive the Graveyard.

I was captivated by the warbirds and was determined to dive as much of the site as possible. Many specific aircraft types had been marked by GPS on a list we kept in the scuba club. I tried to check off every plane. At other times, I dived in areas that were not on the list.

Before I left the atoll, I had dived on all eleven documented PBJ Mitchells, the Helldiver, the C-46, two Avengers, the Corsair, and numerous Wildcats and Douglas Dauntless SBDs. Sites had names like "Three Planes," where there were three SBDs close together. It wasn't all aircraft either. There were also a few tanks, lots of badly rusted Jeeps and truck chassis, piles of dumped .50 caliber bullets, and a variety of other stray munitions.

Many of the planes I had never seen before in anything other than pictures and a few museum exhibits in the Smithsonian or elsewhere. I thought of the lagoon as an underwater museum, except that instead of one or two aircraft, there were 150, give or take. That was beyond museum

Three Douglas Dauntles SBDs

Grey reef shark under the wing of a PBJ-1 Mitchell

numbers, and it made me think of the tremendous resources dedicated to fighting the Pacific war. I never even knew I was an airplane enthusiast. I certainly never thought I'd be much interested in World War II history. These obsessions sort of snuck up on me.

I learned to look and to see the different aircraft underwater, noting differences between the types and even between examples of the same type. As a marine biologist, you learn to observe, noting the little things and asking questions about what they mean. Back on the surface, I'd follow up my firsthand aircraft observations with the internet. When I became impatient with the glacial tempo of the island's digital connections, I'd pump my airplane guru friends. Then I branched out to the WWII shipwrecks and set out to learn more about the war fought out among so many of the islands I loved to dive.

The obvious attractions of the tropical Pacific are, well, obvious. Boundless beauty, sunshine, beaches, azure

Tiny fish living around a Wildcat

skies and waters. I learned to embrace the subtle and the hidden—the violent past, the haunting, compelling scars of war, whether overgrown by jungle, submerged with striking clarity in the lagoon, or covered in coral. The people who live here live with the past and tell the stories of war and defeat and victory. They tell stories of the Airplane Graveyard.

iscarded shells on the wing of the Helldiver

A diver on the C-46

The skeleton of a vehicle also
dumped in the graveyard

The grill of a Jeep or a truck in the graveyard

Looking up at Kwajalein Atoll from below

The small boat dock where we load scuba tanks

CHAPTER 2
DIVING THE WRECKS

What a strange thing, seeing airplanes underwater. You expect ships to end up underwater someday. Challenge nature by riding the sea, and you chance being swallowed. But planes belong in the air. True, what goes up must come down to earth again, and seventy-one percent of the planet is covered by water. That some aircraft will end up under the sea is inevitable. Yet, the sight of submerged aircraft, arrested in time, seems almost mystical to me. In other words, the Airplane Graveyard of Kwajalein Atoll is mind-blowing for a scuba diver.

On a morning like many others on Roi-Namur—Roi for short—a few of my dive buddies and I head out into the lagoon in a rented boat. We've biked from our quarters on one side of the island to the marina, dragging behind small trailers filled with scuba gear, cameras, water, snacks, and plenty of sunscreen. There is no wind, and the sun is already unrelenting. Tropical heat and humidity are pretty much a year-round thing on Kwaj, but this is summer, the doldrums, in which wind is a rarity. The celebrated trade winds of this part of the world are creatures of the winter months, and they feel welcome—though they make it harder to pedal a bike and they can whip up enough waves to make diving impossible. So, today, we try not to complain about the heat. Anyway, we'll be underwater soon.

We load the boat with dive and emergency gear: GPS, marine radio, life jackets, first aid kit, fire extinguisher, and a pair of paddles. We drive the loaded boat to a small dock on the other side of the harbor and load up scuba tanks. If you think serious (as in living) divers are happy-go-lucky and devil-may-care, you would revise your thinking if you saw us double-check everything before setting off on the dive. Right now, each of us wants to avoid embarrassment. Forget a mask, and you'll not only miss out on diving, you'll

The road to the boat marina on Roi

endure jokes at your expense that won't end until someone else does something worthy of new jokes. But the checking and double-checking are part of an awareness that, underwater, life depends on your gear and your vigilance.

The wind stirred by the speeding boat feels great. After about twenty minutes, I slow down as we approach the dive site. Once we are over the point marked on the GPS, we throw in an anchor. That secured, we throw another, which we will set once we are underwater, to make sure the boat doesn't drift away and run aground on the nearby reef while we are below.

Gear on, I sit on the edge of the boat. With one hand, I hold my regulator in my mouth and my mask in place. My other hand is behind my head for protection. I look behind me once more to make sure it is clear back there, and I

How I transported my dive gear

back-roll off the six-passenger boat and into the bathwater-warm lagoon. The temperature is only a slight relief from the punishingly hot equatorial air.

Our successive splashes ripple the still water. Once everyone has signaled okay, we start our descent together, letting air out of our buoyancy-control devices to slowly sink into the blue. The clear water is lit by sunshine even as we make our way to one hundred feet (thirty meters). I scan the area for a shadow—anything different from blue. As we near the sand, I see off in the distance the shadow I'm looking for. Pointing, I turn to my buddies, who are also pointing. They've spotted it, too.

We go deeper and toward the shadow, which gradually morphs into the shape of a nose-down airplane. It looks as if it crashed straight up and down into the ocean floor, propeller dug into the sand. From the looks of it, the "crash" could have happened yesterday. The aircraft is in fantastic condition—very much intact.

Why? Because it did not crash—not yesterday and not some seven decades ago. It was dumped from a barge.

Today, we are diving one of the most popular planes in the Airplane Graveyard, the Vought F4U Corsair. During its production, which began with prototypes in 1940 and

ended in 1953 when final models were delivered to the French, 12,571 F4Us were manufactured. Yet this is the only Corsair in the graveyard. Fortunately, because it landed nose down in the soft sand and in a spot where there is nothing but clear water and clean sand as far as the eye can see, it is among the most photogenic planes.

We get closer. Looking down from the tail, we see that the wings are bent a little and curved upward. This isn't damage. The F4U wing is a gently inverted "gull-wing," which allowed engineers to design short landing gear, sturdy enough to take the repeated punishment of hard pancake landings on the limited space of an aircraft carrier. The gull shape also allowed the wings to be folded up more easily. Even in World War II, aircraft carriers were big ships, but space was nevertheless at a premium. Folding wings were indispensable to efficiently storing aircraft, whether on deck or on the hangar deck below.

After some seventy years in salt water, this Corsair has suffered astoundingly little erosion of the aluminum, although some of it is blanketed in a lichen-like sponge, yellow or red wherever you shine a light on it. Incongruously, a spare propeller sits in the cockpit where a pilot should be. This is a common feature of a lot of the planes in the graveyard. Presumably, the props were taken off many of the planes to make them easier to load for their final voyage on the funeral barge. The prop on this aircraft, however, was not removed. It is partly buried in the sand. The one it carries in its cockpit belongs to some other plane or was a spare part deemed trash in October 1945.

The cockpit and the area surrounding the spare propeller are covered with schooling glassfish, tiny, orange, swarming so tightly that they block the view of whatever is behind them. They are a moving curtain. Sweep your hand near them, and they move away in perfect unison, only to

coalesce again as soon as your hand is gone. Then there are the lionfish, incredibly showy in red and white and black with spiky, venomous fin rays. They love areas where propellers are in the sand. Three or four can almost always be seen, sometimes resting right on the prop blades. When they get hungry, they move upward just a bit to partake in the cockpit buffet of glassfish.

For scuba diving there is a maximum bottom time you can stay at certain depths without doing decompression stops. Such stops are rigorous routine in the realm of technical diving, but they are not something a recreational diver usually does and, in any case, for safety reasons, they are not permitted for employees working on Kwajalein. We wear dive computers that tell us how much longer we can stay at any particular depth. Our time has quickly counted down. At one hundred feet, a diver has just twenty minutes before going into "deco," which requires stopping at specified depths

Right and Below: Lionfish on the Corsair

to off-gas excess nitrogen before returning to the surface. There are more planes near the Corsair, but most are a good five minute swim away or longer. We've spent almost all our bottom time on the Corsair, and our computers are telling us it is time to start going shallower. So, we swim a little way up the sand slope close to the barrier reef and see two

SBD Douglas Dauntless aircraft sitting upright in the sand at about sixty feet. One is mostly buried, probably due to sand shifting during strong weather. Yet it is one of the planes down here that makes me think you could just brush off the sand, start it up, and take off—returning to the sky directly from the lagoon floor.

Douglas Dauntless partially buried in the sand

It's a nice thought, but we continue our ascent, stopping at fifteen feet for a three-minute safety stop to reduce the likelihood of decompression sickness, the infamous "bends," caused by dissolved gases coming out in bubbles inside the body and bloodstream if you decompress too rapidly. Symptoms range from pain to death and a lot of other bad things in between those extremes. The three minutes are well worth it. Even after that time passes, we make our way to the surface and the sunshine unhurriedly.

THE AVENGER

Over the last few years, several news outlets have misreported that I "discovered" the Airplane Graveyard. Obviously, I did no such thing. The site has been well known to people living on Kwaj since the planes were dumped in 1945, and divers have visited at least as far back as the 1960s. True, the difficulty of gaining access to the diving in Kwajalein Atoll has kept many away. But the graveyard is not a secret.

While I never claimed to have discovered the Airplane Graveyard, there is one plane there to which I *might* have a discovery claim. I may not have been the first to see it—I don't know—but it was not recorded on the extensive GPS listing maintained by the Roi Dolphins Scuba Club. My friend Dan and I came across it when we were diving between my scheduled ferry runs. My shift schedule imposed a hard limit on how long we could be out. It was a little windier than we'd have liked. In fact, a smarter pair would probably not have been diving that area in those conditions because the wind made the water choppy. Since the graveyard area is mostly sand, anchoring the boat securely can be iffy, particularly on choppy days.

Dan and I had been on a mission to dive all spots in the GPS-listed graveyard, and that day we chose a mark neither of us had been to. I was driving the boat, pulled up to the spot, and Dan threw the anchor. Then we waited. And waited. We watched the GPS to see if our distance from the target moved, indicating that we had not hooked the anchor and were being dragged by the wind. Most of the airplanes are very close to the shallow barrier reef encircling the lagoon. If the boat drifted while the divers were underwater and ran aground on the reef, that would be a bad thing for many reasons. In this case, the most significant peril I could

think of was not getting back to the ferry on time.

According to the GPS, we were slowly moving farther away from our target, 100 feet, 150 … 200. The GPS kept going. I had Dan hoist the anchor, and I drove back to the GPS mark. He threw the anchor again, and we waited. And, again, the GPS moved. Time was ticking. The more time we spent hooking up, the less of it we had to dive. Not wanting to haul up the anchor again, we kept waiting. At about 400 feet, the GPS stopped. We both looked at it and looked at each other. Well, we could swim 400 feet, right? That wasn't too far.

In fact, it was quite far, especially where we were going to dive, an area subject to strong currents during tidal changes—something we hadn't checked before coming out. Impatience, however, is a powerful driver. Frustrated with the sand, frustrated with the wind, we were also frustrated with one another. The decision? Just go for it.

We took a compass heading on the direction toward where the plane was supposed to be, 400 feet behind us, and we jumped in. Maybe we would find it. Maybe not. Either way, we were finally diving, and diving is always better than working.

Being a boat captain—and having signed my name to the reservation for this rented boat—I felt a slight twinge of nerves about leaving it alone in the wind. But these dives were usually around 100 feet, so we'd be underwater for eighteen to twenty minutes tops before our bottom time ran out. It didn't seem like too much could go wrong in that span.

Generally, the air temperature on Kwaj stays constant at eighty-five degrees, but the wind that day made it slightly chilly, and the water, at eighty-two, actually felt warmer than the air as we began our descent. We started out facing each other, and even though we needed to start swimming southeast, we also needed, first thing, to check that the anchors were secure at the bottom. Following the anchor lines down, we were at about thirty feet, still right under the boat, when I saw a shadow.

A plane!

But, clearly, it wasn't the plane, the one we were looking for—unless the GPS coordinates we had were incorrect. Either way, it was a plane we had never seen. So, we quickly checked the anchors, repositioned them securely, and headed to the plane.

This dive was still quite early in my graveyard adventures, so I wasn't up on my aircraft recognition. I had no idea what type of plane I was looking at, but I did know that I really liked the look of it, sitting upright in the sand on the slope down from the reef. The engine was broken off, positioned just in front of the fuselage, although mostly buried in the sand. The tips of the wings were also buried, but I could see that the wings were partly folded, so it had to be a carrier-based aircraft.

There was nothing but white sand all around. The cockpit was so thickly filled with glassfish that you couldn't see the instrument panel without shooing them away. Whip corals, long, thin, and greenish, looking like long pipe cleaners, grew off the aircraft. There were crinoids, too, one of those sea animals that look like plants—or, in this case, like feather dusters, which is what most people call them. Their feather-like leaves ball up into a sphere and can be black, yellow, or many other colors besides green. Moorish idols, in bold white, black, and yellow, and emperor angelfish, vibrant in yellow horizontal pinstripes on a blue background, swam around the plane along with many other less showy fish species.

We also swam around this plane a few times, and when we'd seen enough we still had some bottom time left. So, we signaled to each other that we should swim farther in hopes of finding the plane we were looking for—or maybe something else. We used our compasses to swim in the direction we had originally intended. After a while, having come across nothing and with our bottom time running out, it was time to start heading to shallower waters. The current had also picked up, moving us farther away from the boat, so we started kicking harder to get back to the anchor line.

Reaching the line, we ascended, did our three-minute safety stop, and returned to the surface. Thankfully, the boat was still there. Our excitement—especially after that rough start—was hard to hold back. We were still unsure if what we had seen was the plane we were after or something else altogether. Either way, we were happy we had found something.

I told Dan we should mark the GPS and jokingly suggested we call it "Brandi's Plane." He protested mildly, saying that he was sure it had to be on the list somewhere and that we must have just drifted over to another spot. But, in the end, grudgingly, he put the coordinates in, and, bringing the boat back to shore, we were all smiles. I did my ferry run

and then scurried back to my room to download the photos. I posted one on Facebook.

Minutes—and I mean minutes—after I posted, the undisputed "WWII Airplane Guru" of Kwajalein posted a comment in response. He identified the aircraft as a Grumman TBF Avenger, a torpedo bomber developed for the U.S. Navy and Marine Corps. Like the other warbirds in the graveyard, the Avenger was a hero of World War II. It first flew on August 7, 1941 and made its combat debut at the Battle of Midway (June 4-7, 1942). Five of the six that flew during that fight were lost. But Midway nevertheless turned the tide against Japan in the Pacific war, and the Avenger went on to become the premier torpedo bomber of World War II.

As for me, the Guru commented that the only other Graveyard Avenger he knew about was upside down in the sand. This really got me excited, and Dan and I asked every diver on Roi if they had ever seen or heard about an *upright* Avenger. No one had.

Did this mean that Dan and I were the first human beings to dive it? Common sense tells me that someone at some time saw it but just didn't mark it. Well, we marked it. So, if I can take credit for finding anything, I'll take it for this plane.

Right: The plane we saw

Above: The nose was broken off and laying in the sand in front of it

Exploring the Avenger

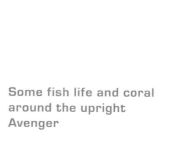

Some fish life and coral
around the upright
Avenger

RACHEL'S BOMBER

On another day, Dan and I—with two other divers, Rachel and John—decided to tick off one of the PBJ-1 Mitchells on the GPS list. These aircraft are Navy and Marine Corps versions of the immortal B-25 Mitchell medium bombers flown by the U.S. Army Air Forces. The "P" stands for Patrol, indicating that the planes were used extensively to patrol for enemy ships, especially submarines. The "B" stands for Bomber, and the "J" is the USN/USMC designation for aircraft built by North American Aviation. The "1" signified that it was the first variant on the original North American design. The Marine Corps, not the Navy, was the principal user of the land-based PBJs, and all eleven recorded in the graveyard—though only nine were catalogued on the scuba club's GPS list—were flown by the Marines.

They are really great to dive because they are the second-largest aircraft in the graveyard and usually very full of marine life. All but one sits upright in the sand, which is a properly dignified way for a great airplane to be seen, but the one PBJ that is upside down in its Kwajalein grave is even more exciting because the bomb bay doors are wide open and you can see up—or, actually, down—into the belly of the beast.

We threw over the anchor, which didn't catch until it was some 250 feet off the target. So, we took a compass heading before jumping in. As the four of us descended, I saw something off in the distance, in the direction opposite our heading. I turned around and saw that Rachel saw it, too. We both pointed, getting the attention of the boys and motioning that we wanted to go that way.

Dan and John preferred to continue to the compass heading. Through hand signals, we decided that Rachel and I would split off. While we headed toward the shadow, the boys continued to the originally targeted area. Our shadow turned out to be a nose-down SBD with wings attached. In the main graveyard site, none of the nose-down SBDs have their wings attached. In the distance, I could barely make out another SBD, also nose down. Both of these planes were great for photos, and I snapped away as we moved from one to the next. We came across a third nose-down SBD, so that all three were in a row.

Then I saw a much larger plane in the sand just beyond the third SBD. Once we got closer, it became clear that

Nose down SBD with wings attached

here was another PBJ. This confounded us because the PBJ marked on the club's GPS list was supposed to be in the opposite direction. It crossed my mind that maybe this was the one we were looking for but the coordinates were off. I wondered if the boys might have found nothing at all.

"Our" PBJ sat upright in the sand, directly facing an SBD that was also upright. It looked as if the two planes were in a faceoff. On size alone, the PBJ would clearly win the encounter. This PBJ had the ladder to the flight deck down, something I hadn't seen on any other PBJ aircraft.

Our bottom time was running out, and we had a long swim back. We slowly started to ascend while backtracking past the three nose-down SBDs until we could see our anchor line and the boys on their safety stop at fifteen feet. Joining them and completing our stop, we all went to the surface together.

The PBJ facing an SBD

Left: The ladder down on the PBJ helped us identify this PBJ as unique

I'm always a bit hesitant about telling others when I see something really cool underwater. I don't want to seem like I'm rubbing anything in, especially if the people I'm talking to haven't found much. So, back on the boat, I reluctantly asked Dan and John if they saw anything.

Yes, they answered. They found the PBJ!

Now I was really confused because it seemed unlikely that two PBJs were that close together without both having been recorded. Moving around underwater can be disorienting, even for experienced divers, and we began to wonder if maybe we all saw the same aircraft and somehow had crossed paths without noticing. I asked about the ladder we saw, and Rachel and I described the nose-down SBDs nearby. Dan and John had seen no ladder and no nose-down SBDs. The idea began to crystallize that there must two PBJs close together and that we had seen different airplanes.

It was either that or one of our duos was swimming in circles and we had all seen the same PBJ.

Because we couldn't be certain that there were two aircraft—one of them unlisted, which would make it one of the two PBJs recorded historically but unaccounted for in the present—we decided to stay put and dive the spot again. After an hour's interval on the surface, mostly devoted to mutual expressions of disbelief and doubt, we jumped back in and headed down to the sand. The plan was to go first to the plane Rachel and I saw. We followed the same path of nose-down SBDs until we got to it. John and Dan looked excited. I could tell that our plane was not theirs. After a few minutes at our PBJ, we took off in the other direction to see theirs. We swam back past the SBDs and our boat's anchor line and after a five-minute swim we saw the PBJ we had originally set out for.

Diver taking photos to later compare PBJs

Left: An inside view of the cockpit of the PBJ

Back on the boat, we talked excitedly about how cool it was to find two PBJs within swimming distance of each other. Back on land, we checked the list again to make sure the one wasn't already on it and there were no other PBJs listed as being so close. Ours was not on the list.

I know that there is a good chance some diver at some time had seen this PBJ. But it had not been recorded. We had taken a GPS point, and a few weeks later went back to the spot and dived. Once we were right on the plane, we sent a weighted line with a safety sausage to the surface. A large orange tube easily inflated with air from a spare regulator, it floats to the surface as the weight at the other end of the line holds it in place at the bottom. When we got back to the surface, we drove the boat directly over the plane and took a GPS reading to fix the exact coordinates for future divers. We named it "Rachel's Bomber" on our plane list. Alas, poor Dan, maybe someday we'll give a plane his name.

OTHER DIVES, OTHER PLANES

I cannot recount all my dives on the Airplane Graveyard, but there are other planes I don't want to fail to mention. There is only one SB2C Helldiver in the graveyard, a carrier-based dive bomber from Curtiss Aviation and kind of an ugly duckling among the warbirds. Pilots and carrier captains alike called the SB2C the "Big-Tailed Beast." This was partly because the plane has a conspicuously oversized tail and partly because those who flew it had little affection for it. The SB2C was notorious for not handling very well, and by the time a host of production problems had been ironed out and the plane was introduced into service in December 1942, improved munitions reduced the demand for dive bombers.

The Airplane Graveyard's Helldiver

Artillery shells on the Helldiver

The graveyard doesn't seem to give the Helldiver a lot of respect. Artillery shells rest unceremoniously on one wing, and the inside of the plane's nose serves as what scuba divers call a "cleaning station." Bluestreak cleaner wrasses, small light-blue fish with a broad dark-blue streak from head to tail, live within. They are textbook examples of symbiosis, feeding on the parasites that afflict other fish. Those fish enter the Helldiver's nose and hold still while wrasses obligingly pick them clean. Sometimes a wrasse even cleans inside their teeth, trusting that the fish won't chomp down and eat it. The fish get cleaned, and the wrasse gets fed. It is the essence of a win-win symbiotic relationship.

An emperor angelfish being cleaned by a bluestreak cleaner wrasse in the Helldiver's nose

The Helldiver came to rest very close to a pass that admits an inflow of clean water from the ocean. This gives the area fantastic visibility but also, at times, a ripping current. Beyond that solitary Helldiver are several F4F Wildcats, mostly with wings folded. These Grumman aircraft first flew in September 1937 and were introduced into the Navy fleet a year before Pearl Harbor, in December 1940. The Wildcat was the best the Navy had at the outbreak of the war in the Pacific, but the Mitsubishi Zero easily outperformed it—except when it came to sheer ruggedness. Its toughness made the Wildcat an effective air weapon, despite its early obsolescence. On one dive, we decided to see how many Wildcats we could count before running out of bottom time. We descended on the Helldiver and started swimming east. I think we got to around seven before having to go back.

Another favorite is the lagoon's one and only C-46. Everybody knows the C-47, a military transport plane developed from the Douglas DC-3 commercial airliner. C-47 production exceeded 10,000 aircraft during the war, far more than the 3,181 C-46 Commandos built by Curtiss. The Navy and Marine version of the plane was designated the R5C. It was a big cargo and troop transport and today, in the graveyard, is home to a great many fish. Its wings were removed before it was dumped into the lagoon, but, elsewhere in the graveyard, we've seen large wings that are likely from this aircraft.

Near the C-46 are several well-rusted Jeeps and truck chassis. These are a reminder that there are more than just planes in the Airplane Graveyard, which has several tanks, a lot of artillery shells and bullets, as well as a wealth of Jeeps, trucks, tires, spare aircraft parts, and other debris.

A diver with two Wildcats

Right: The open door to the cockpit of the C-46

Below: Some of the debris near the C-46

MORE THAN JUST THE AIRPLANE GRAVEYARD

The diving off Roi is not limited to the graveyard. On more than one occasion, my dive buddies groaned at my request to return again and again to look at planes when there was so much else to dive for at Roi. There are three Japanese shipwrecks, vessels sunk in combat during December 1943 or January 1944. Local divers call them First, Second, and Third Ship, but they are properly the *Eiko Maru*, the *Kembu Maru*, and the *Takunan Maru*.

Eiko Maru was heavily damaged by U.S. Navy aircraft on December 4, 1943 and towed to Roi-Namur. Late in January 1944, it was docked off Roi, awaiting a tow to Truk or perhaps to Japan for repairs. The battleship USS *North Carolina* bombarded it with artillery on January 29, scoring a direct hit that sent it to the bottom of the Northern Atoll of Kwaj. Here the water was so shallow that the ship's mast remained above the surface. During the U.S. occupation late in the war, engineers blew off the masts and the funnel to clear the channel of obstacles to navigation.

Above: The bow gun of the *Kembu Maru* is the largest in the lagoon Maru

Right: The bow gun of the *Eiko Maru*

Kembu Maru was also attacked on December 4, 1943 by planes from the aircraft carrier USS *Lexington*. Bombs and torpedoes set off an explosion that produced a column of smoke ten thousand feet high before the ship sank. *Takunan Maru* was attacked by *Lexington* aircraft on December 4 and sank three miles off Roi. Almost all its wooden hull—the *Takunan* was a small, light sub chaser—and superstructure are long gone. Engines, fuel tanks, two six-foot anchors, unexploded depth charges, and other items of equipment are all that remain.

The three ships make for great dives, as all but the *Takunan Maru* are very much intact and home to a dazzling variety of marine life, with corals and sponges growing on the ships and more animated creatures living around and within. Baby sharks are often seen curiously poking around the Eiko, and schools of fusiliers swim by in groups of more than a hundred. Two kingposts reach up from the wreck to about fifteen feet deep, which make them excellent places for safety stops. The stern of the *Kembu* is missing, likely destroyed by burning aviation fuel when it was bombed. Its massive five-inch bow gun is the largest-caliber ship's gun in the lagoon.

Eiko Maru

A diver swims through the remains of a companionway on the *Takunan Maru*

Left: *Eiko Maru*

Japanese Zero off Roi

Airplanes that crashed in combat are also found near Roi-Namur as well as the Southern end of the atoll. Just off the shore of Roi is a Zero. Several undiscovered American and Japanese planes are known to have crashed near here but have yet to be found. Some believe the remains of MIAs are still within them.

Closer to Kwajalein Island, at the south end of the atoll, are more combat casualties, including a Japanese "Jake" and "Mavis." These were code names the Allies gave to the single-engine Aichi E13A long-distance reconnaissance seaplane and the Kawanishi H6K, a large, four-engine flying boat patrol aircraft. In addition to these Japanese wrecks are some large American naval aircraft, three twin-engine Martin Mariner PBM flying boat patrol bombers and two immense four-engine Consolidated Coronados—a PB2Y-3 and a PB2Y-5R. The PB2Y-3 version was a type used for bombing and antisubmarine patrols, and the PB2Y-5R was a type that had been converted for use as a transport, including, in some cases, medical evacuation. Other planes are out there, yet to be found.

Japanese long-range reconnaissance seaplane Aichi E13A "Jake" captured on Kwajalein

Right: Engine of a Japanese Mavis off Ebeye

Many more Japanese warships were sunk during Operation Flintlock. Some have been found and identified. Others have not. But the strangest wreck of all may be the *Prinz Eugen*, a German cruiser launched in 1938 and surrendered to the British Royal Navy after the fall of Nazi Germany in May 1945. The British in turn transferred it to the U.S. Navy, which used it in the July 1946 Operation Crossroads, a pair of nuclear weapons tests conducted in the

Bikini Atoll. *Prinz Eugen* survived both these underwater nuclear bomb detonations, tests designated unimaginatively enough as "Able" and "Baker." Although only lightly damaged, *Prinz Eugen* was contaminated and highly radioactive. It was towed back to Kwajalein Atoll, but when a small leak developed as a result of the July detonations, it could not be repaired because of the radiation danger.

Martin Mariner PBM

The propellers of the *Prinz Eugen*

By December, five months after the leak was discovered, *Prinz Eugen* began listing severely. It was being towed out of the lagoon to be dumped oceanside when, on December 22, it capsized off Carlson (or Enubuj) Island. There it rests to this day, in the sand, almost completely upside down, two of its propellers sticking partly out of the water (The third propeller, removed in August 1979, is at the German Naval Memorial at Laboe in Schleswig-Holstein, Germany). After the Airplane Graveyard, the *Prinz Eugen* wreck is one of the best dives in the Atoll.

The *Prinz Eugen* from the air

Two U.S. Marine Corps Vought F4U-1A Corsair aircraft from Marine Fighting Squadron VMF-113 in flight near Eniwetok. (Public Domain)

CHAPTER 3
OPERATION FLINTLOCK

People on Kwajalein remember. Today, a plaque on Kwajalein Island commemorates—

Operation Flintlock

31 January—4 February 1944

In memory of the 332 American service members who gave their lives for the causes of freedom and democracy in Operation Flintlock, the battles for Kwajalein and Roi Namur.

The inscription concludes with something President John F. Kennedy said in his 1961 inaugural address: "Let every nation know, whether it wishes us well or ill, that we shall pay any price, bear any burden, meet any hardship, support any friend, oppose any foe, to assure the survival and success of liberty."

THE DECISION TO INVADE KWAJALEIN AND ENIWETOK

At the beginning of World War II in the Pacific, the Marshall Islands, 2,449 miles from Pearl Harbor in Hawaii, was part of the outer defensive perimeter of Japan's Pacific empire. Before 1943 ended, the Americans would fully turn the tide of the Pacific war against Japan.

It began with victory at Midway in July 1942 and at Guadalcanal by the end of that year. On February 8, 1943, the Japanese completed their withdrawal from Guadalcanal, and on April 18, acting on intercepted Japanese radio traffic, American commanders learned that Admiral Isoroku Yamamoto, architect of the December 7, 1941 attack on Pearl Harbor, was touring Japanese bases on Shortland Island in a bomber. Fighter aircraft were dispatched to shoot down the aircraft transporting him. Yamamoto's death was more than sweet revenge for Pearl Harbor. It took Japan's best naval strategist out of the Pacific war.

Throughout the rest of 1943, Americans took New Georgia and Bougainville in the Solomon Islands and Tarawa in the Gilberts. As the year waned, Mineichi Koga, admiral of the Japanese Combined Fleet, became acutely aware that the Americans were likely to move next against the Marshalls. His first problem was figuring out where they would strike. His second problem was devising a way to counter that strike. His aircraft carriers were critically short of airplanes, many of which had been transferred to island land bases, which were in urgent need of reinforcement. Koga temporized by sending his submarines to do remote reconnaissance, and, in the meantime, he ordered the regional commander, headquartered at Truk (Chuuk), Admiral Masashi Kobayashi, to reinforce those of his island garrisons most obviously vulnerable to American attack. Accordingly, Kobayashi shifted men to the outer islands in the Marshall group, Jaluit, Mili, Maloelap, and Wotje. With just 28,000 troops available to him, he knew that his forces would be outnumbered. Moreover, he knew that the fortifications on these islands would not provide effective defensive protection for very long. But he also knew that Japanese high command in Tokyo no longer expected the empire's outer perimeter to last forever. The strategy now was to delay the Americans and take a toll on them in a bid to buy time for Japanese forces to create a new defensive perimeter much closer to the home island.

Even before Pearl Harbor, American military intelligence officers had broken key Imperial Japanese Navy codes. Admiral Chester W. Nimitz, commander of the U.S. Pacific Fleet, acted on intercepted and decrypted Japanese radio messages in combination with aerial observation of troop movements to the outer islands. Nimitz had intended to focus an attack on these very islands. What he decrypted and what he saw prompted him to change his invasion plans. He would now largely bypass the outer islands, reinforced as they were, and instead invade Kwajalein and Eniwetok directly.

TAKING MAJURO

Vice Admiral John Howard Hoover, in command of land-based aircraft in the Central Pacific sector, used four-engine B-24 Liberator bombers and other 7th U.S. Army Air Forces attack aircraft based at Ellice and Gilbert Islands to bomb Mili and Maloelap islands in November 1943. This was a feint designed to deceive the Japanese into thinking that the main attack would, in fact, descend upon the outer islands. On December 3, Rear Admiral Charles Pownall's Task Force 50 launched an aircraft carrier strike against Kwajalein Atoll, combining aircraft from four huge fleet carriers and two smaller light carriers.

Although the strike destroyed four transports and fifty Japanese aircraft, it did not make much of a strategic dent.

Worse, it exposed the American carriers to a Japanese counterattack, which was launched from the airfield at Wotje—at night. The timing was bad because American carrier pilots were not trained for night flying and therefore could not defend their ships. USS *Lexington* suffered an aerial torpedo hit but survived.

In the meantime, Majuro Atoll was selected as a forward base to be used in preparation for the invasion. Rear Admiral Harry Hill landed the Reconnaissance Company of the U.S. Marines V Amphibious Corps along with the 2nd Battalion of the 106th Infantry Regiment of the U.S. Army's 7th Infantry Division on the atoll, which was so lightly defended that the objective fell on January 31 without any American casualties.

A U.S. Navy SOC Seagull floatplane flies over Wotje Atoll, during the attack on the Japanese airfield there on February 1, 1942. (Public Domain)

MAJURO TO ROI-NAMUR

Despite the ease with which Majuro was taken, logistical hiccups delayed the step-off from Majuro to Kwajalein Atoll a full month. Nimitz was having difficulty assembling the required fleet of troop transports, but once he had scraped the necessary ships together, he wasted no time in launching the main phase of Operation Flintlock, which targeted Kwajalein followed by Eniwetok.

Rear Admiral Richmond Turner commanded the forces assigned to take Kwajalein Island in the south. His transports carried Major General Charles Corlett's U.S. Army 7th Infantry Division. Simultaneously, in the north, Rear Admiral Richard Connolly would land the 4th Marine Division under Major General Harry Schmidt on Roi-Namur. A third task force, commanded by Rear Admiral Harry Hill, served as a reserve force prepared to assist either of the two principal invasion forces.

Amphibious operations in World War II covered more than water and land. Vice Admiral Marc Mitscher commanded six fleet carriers and six light carriers escorted by eight battleships and the usual contingent of cruisers and destroyers. This fleet steamed into position to launch the extensive air coverage that would accompany the action at sea and on land.

On paper, Admiral Kobayashi had a garrison of 8,000 distributed across the Kwajalein Atoll. However, only half this number were combat soldiers. The rest were conscripts and aircraft ground support personnel as well as forced laborers, mostly Koreans. The ground commander, Rear Admiral Monzo Akiyama, headquartered on Kwajalein Island, was very aware of his troop shortages as well as the vulnerability of his fortifications. He intended, however, to use his air assets to mount a credible aerial counterattack against the invasion forces.

On January 29, 1944, U.S. carrier planes targeted Japanese aircraft based at Roi-Namur. One hundred ten planes survived American pre-invasion strikes, which had been made during November and December 1943. The air assault of January 29 annihilated ninety-two of these—on the ground. Suddenly, the air arm Akiyama had counted on was gone. He was powerless to counterattack the invasion.

Two days later, on January 31, the invasion itself got underway against Roi-Namur. The first objectives were landings on five small islands near Roi. The next day, February 1, however, bad weather combined with the relative inexperience of Schmidt's marines in carrying out complex amphibious operations created both confusion and delay. It was lucky for the Americans that Japanese resistance on Roi was much lighter than anticipated. The pre-invasion bombardment from aircraft and naval artillery had taken a heavier than expected toll, reducing the Japanese garrison on Roi-Namur to just 300 men. By the time the fight for the island was over, a mere fifty-one Japanese soldiers remained alive. The original strength of the garrison had been 3,000. The marines lost 172 men killed in action, with an additional eighteen later dying from their wounds. Five hundred forty-seven marines were wounded and recovered.

Official U.S. Navy photo of the invasion of Roi-Namur. Navy assault landing craft approach Namur (center) and Roi (right) Islands, Kwajalein Atoll. (Public Domain)

INVADING KWAJ

The invasion of Kwajalein Atoll began on January 31 in much the same way as the operations against Roi-Namur were carried out. That is, the first phase was the capture of smaller outlying islands in the atoll for use as platforms from which the major landings would be launched. The movement from the outer islands to the major islands on February 1 went much more efficiently than the main landings on Roi. The Army's 7th Infantry Division was unloaded on Kwajalein Island—men, vehicles, and equipment—swiftly and against relatively little resistance. The Japanese had anticipated that any American landing would have to be made on the ocean side of Kwaj rather than on the reef side. They did not know that the American forces had shallow-draft landing craft capable of traversing coral reefs. The 7th Infantry therefore landed *behind* the Japanese defenders. Moreover, they landed *after* American ships and aircraft had thoroughly bombarded the garrison positions. As British Royal Navy observer Commander Anthony

Japanese ships under attack in Kwajalein lagoon as seen from a U.S. Navy Consolidated PB4Y-1 Liberator, circa December 1943 (Public Domain)

Kimmins later remarked, "Nothing could have lived through that sea and air bombardment." He called it "the most damaging thing" he had ever seen, recounting that the shore was a "shambles...the beach...a mass of highly colored fish that had been thrown up there by nearby explosions." In all, it was "the most brilliant success" he had ever seen.

Akiyama's garrison was able to counterattack on the ground and did so ferociously, pushing back against the advance of the 7th Infantry. Yet, by dawn on February 2, only 1,500 of the original 5,000-man Japanese garrison were alive. By the end of that day, when Kwajelein Island had been secured, only 265 Japanese soldiers were captured as prisoners. Astounding as this butcher's bill is, it was typical of the Pacific war. Japanese soldiers and sailors did not surrender. They died.

On the American side, 142 troops of the 7th Infantry were killed in action and 845 were wounded.

INVADING ENIWETOK

The invasion of the Eniwetok Atoll is associated with Operation Flintlock, although it was carried out during February 17-21, more than two weeks after the operation formally ended. Its objective, a collection of small islands and even smaller islets, some forty in all, totaled a bit more than two square miles of land. The point, however, was that these two square miles were strategically critical. They would serve as platforms for airfields from which the aerial component of the next invasion, against the Marianas, would be launched.

The Japanese commander, Major General Yoshimi Nishida, appreciated as fully as his American counterparts the strategic importance of little Eniwetok. During 1943, he had overseen a build-up of defenses of the main island, Eniwetok. But defending a small island is not easy. Effective defensive practice calls for defense in depth, a defense that requires an attacker to penetrate the first line of defenders only to be swallowed up in subsequent layers of defense. Eniwetok Island was simply too small for such depth. Nishida knew that the only way to stop an invasion was to kill the invaders on the beaches, before they ventured inland. To accomplish this, Nishida had 4,000 men on Eniwetok Island, half Imperial Army, half Imperial Navy.

The effects of Naval bombardment can be seen in this photo of Kwajalein, after its capture on February 4, 1944

The invasion of Eniwetok, like that of Kwajalein, was part of Operation Flintlock, but it had its own name as well: Operation Catchpole. It started with a naval bombardment on February 17, while 8,000 Marines and 2,000 Army infantrymen watched from the decks of their transports. As Eniwetok Island was being shelled, the 22nd Marine Regiment under Colonel John Walker landed on Engebi Island, on the northern side of the Eniwetok Atoll. At first, it did not go well at all. Poor logistical planning meant that the landing of equipment and vehicles was uncoordinated with the landing of Marines. Nevertheless, the landing was made, and the island was secured—by the very next day, February 18, the cost was eighty-five Marines killed in action and another 521 wounded. Japanese losses were 1,276 killed. Only sixteen prisoners were alive to be taken.

On February 19, the Army's 106th Infantry Regiment landed on Eniwetok Island following an all-too-brief naval bombardment, which, unsurprisingly, had not been very effective. Soldiers were caught in a crossfire of Japanese automatic weapons as they traversed the landing beaches. In the hail of bullets, men and vehicles tripped all over each other, lengthening the troops' exposure to the deadly crossfire. Yet, Eniwetok Island was completely secured by February 21, at a loss of thirty-seven U.S. soldiers versus almost the entire Japanese garrison of 800 men.

Casualties on Eniwetok island were small: one killed and one wounded. This is the first, and only, wave to go ashore on the island (Public Domain)

Four U.S. Navy Douglas SBD-5 Dauntless bombers fly over the northern part of Eniwetok Atoll, on February 18, 1944. (Public Domain)

FINAL MOVES

Leaving the army to occupy Eniwetok Island, the 22nd Marine Regiment continued to a landing on Parry Island. Here, the battleships *Tennessee* and *Pennsylvania* unloaded on Japanese defenders some 900 tons of high-explosive ordnance *before* the Marines hit the beach. This averted the logistical problems suffered on Eniwetok Island, and the Marines occupied Parry by February 21, thus concluding Operation Flintlock a spectacular ten weeks ahead of schedule. With this victory, the Marshall Islands, at the outermost perimeter of Japanese strength in the Central Pacific, were now in American hands. Engineers were immediately put to work building the infrastructure of forward bases from which the next phase of the "island hopping" Pacific strategy of Admiral Nimitz and General Douglas MacArthur would proceed to advance, inexorably, toward the Japanese home islands.

Douglas SBD Dauntless in flight. (Public Domain)

CHAPTER 4
DAUNTLESS: "SLOW BUT DEADLY"

Douglas SBD Dauntless

Crew: 2

Length: 33 ft 1¼ in (10.09 m)

Wingspan: 41 ft 6⅜ in (12.66 m)

Height: 13 ft 7 in (4.14 m)

Empty weight: 6,404 lb (2,905 kg)

Loaded weight: 9,359 lb (4,245 kg)

Powerplant: 1 × Wright R-1820-60 radial engine, 1,200 hp (895 kW)

Maximum speed: 255 mph (222 knots, 410 km/h) at 14,000 ft (4,265 m)

Cruise speed: 185 mph (161 knots, 298 km/h)

Range: 1,115 mi (970 nmi, 1,795 km)

Service ceiling: 25,530 ft (7,780 m)

Rate of climb: 1,700 ft/min (8.6 m/s)

Guns: 2 × 0.50 in (12.7 mm) forward-firing synchronized Browning M2 machine guns in front

2 × 0.30 in (7.62 mm) flexible-mounted Browning machine guns in rear

Bombload: 2,250 lb (1,020 kg)

"A military aircraft is built differently than a civilian plane," a Pacific war veteran Dauntless SBD pilot told air war historian Eric M. Bergerud. "They're made to do very demanding maneuvers: an upside-down spin, barrel rolls, anything you can think of. You'd get up to 10,000 feet, dive out, and put stress on a military plane that no civilian pilot in a private plane would dream of—they'd simply come apart. When you're in that power dive you hear that Wright radial just a-hammering out there—it's so noisy in the cockpit because it's being blown right back at you." Then he added: "After a bomb run it was very pleasant in the cockpit. When you pulled out of the dive and cleared the target my gunner and I would light a cigar. You were still alive and had no reason to take it home. It's warm and you're perspiring. In a very few seconds you're coming from about 1,500 to 2,500 feet and the temperature changes a lot. So, the SBD was a workhorse. It would come home with huge holes in the wings and pieces shot off all over. She was a real workhorse, a gorgeous airplane, and I was very lucky to fly it."

Yet when the Dauntless entered service in 1940, most Navy aviators agreed that it was already obsolescent. With a cruise speed of 185 mph and a maximum speed of 255, it was readily outperformed by the infamous Japanese Zero (Mitsubishi A6M), which topped out at nearly 350 mph and was more maneuverable. In fact, the design of the Dauntless went all the way back to 1934, the year Northrop's most brilliant aeronautical engineer, Ed Heinemann, began designing what was at the time a revolutionary carrier-launched dive bomber. In the 1930s, the prevailing technology still employed a great deal of wood and fabric in aircraft skin, and many single-engine military aircraft were biplanes. Heinemann was creating a sleek, all-metal stressed-skin monoplane. It was the future, and in February 1936, the Navy placed the first volume orders for what was then designated the BT-1. Late in the initial production run, the design was improved as the BT-2 and then re-designated the SBD-1 when Northrop Aviation became a subsidiary of the Douglas Aircraft Company.

"SBD" was the Navy and Marine Corps designation for "Scout Bomber Douglas," but pilots, who initially scorned its performance as trailing-edge, began to swear the initials signified *Slow But Deadly*.

Diver examines two SBDs

Before it earned this nickname, the days of the Dauntless were numbered even before they properly began. Recognizing its performance limitations, at least based on its paper specs, the Navy had already ordered a successor, the SB2C Helldiver, but design and production delays dictated that the Dauntless would remain the go-to dive bomber on U.S. Navy fleet carriers until the middle of 1943.

Even after mid-1943, the Dauntless continued to serve on the smaller escort carriers and on land to the very end of the war (Fleet carriers, such as the USS *Lexington*, carried eighty-eight aircraft; escort carriers carried between twenty-eight and thirty-four). Between 1941 and 1942, the heyday of the Dauntless, a typical Navy carrier air group included a scout squadron and a dive-bombing squadron. Each of these consisted of eighteen Dauntless aircraft. Those planes assigned to the scout squadron flew tactical reconnaissance missions, looking for ships and other targets "over the horizon." The scouts almost always flew in pairs for mutual protection. The versatile SBD also populated the carrier's dive-bombing squadron, again, typically, with eighteen planes.

Deemed nothing more than a make-do, a stopgap before the Helldiver was ready for service, the Dauntless surprised everyone by proving itself a highly proficient ship killer. In fact, these planes were credited with sending some 300,000 tons of shipping to the bottom. Among this toll were eighteen Japanese warships, including six aircraft carriers.

Two Dauntless squadrons were deployed in what was arguably the single most decisive Pacific naval battle of World War II, Midway (June 4-7, 1942). That engagement had not begun well for the Americans. The U.S. fleet launched several air attacks against the Japanese fleet with almost nothing to show for it except substantial losses. The Americans'

Diver on SBD

Douglas TBD Devastator torpedo bombers were being shot out of the skies. Of forty-one launched during the Battle of Midway, none scored so much as one torpedo hit and only six survived to return to their carriers. But it was just as Japanese shipboard anti-aircraft gunners and fighter pilots were attacking the few remaining Devastators—now fleeing over the wave tops—that lookouts on the aircraft carrier *Akagi* saw the SBDs incoming.

The time was 10:22 in the morning of June 4, 1942. Forty-eight Dauntless dive bombers were about to change history. Twenty-five of them, SBD-3s, launched from the USS *Enterprise*, dived on the carrier *Kaga*, scoring four direct hits. Within seconds, another six of the *Enterprise* aircraft fell upon on the *Akagi*, hitting it in two places with 1,000-pound bombs. While these attacks were in progress, seventeen SBD-3s from USS *Yorktown* hit another aircraft carrier, the *Soryu*. Three 1,000-pound bombs crashed through its flight deck.

A total of four minutes out of a four-year war in the Pacific ended Japanese domination of that ocean. Three Imperial Navy fleet aircraft carriers, ships that had been instrumental in the attack on Pearl Harbor, were now aflame and sinking. Later that same afternoon, thirteen SBDs from the *Enterprise*—including ten that had been transferred to it from the fatally stricken Yorktown—located a fourth Japanese carrier, the *Hiryu*, and sent it to the bottom with four direct thousand-pound bomb hits. That very night, Japan's Pacific fleet commander, Admiral Isoroku Yamamoto, ordered the surviving ships at Midway to immediately withdraw from the battle area.

In a very real sense, the "Slow But Deadly" Dauntless put the Pacific war on a whole new course, forcing the Japanese Imperial Navy to relinquish the offensive and, for the rest of the

Nose down with wings removed you can still see the tailhook

war, fight an increasingly desperate defense in a long retreat toward Japan itself.

x explains the "Deadly" in the SBD formula. But as historian Bergerud learned, the SBD was also a life saver—for its crews. It would absorb incredible damage—"huge holes in the wings and pieces shot off all over"—but nevertheless "would come home." The Dauntless boasted the lowest loss rate of any U.S. Navy aircraft flown in World War II. Its flight characteristics were extremely stable, which aircrews loved. Unlike larger, later-generation dive bombers, it had lightweight multicell wings that could not be folded. So, the plane had to be small enough to store on an aircraft carrier without hogging too much space. Its size had the added benefit of increasing maneuverability. Although it was designed as a dive bomber, the Dauntless was sufficiently agile enough to be used as a low-level fighter—a role it had performed against Japanese torpedo bombers at the Battle of the Coral Sea (May 4-8, 1942).

Upside down SBD

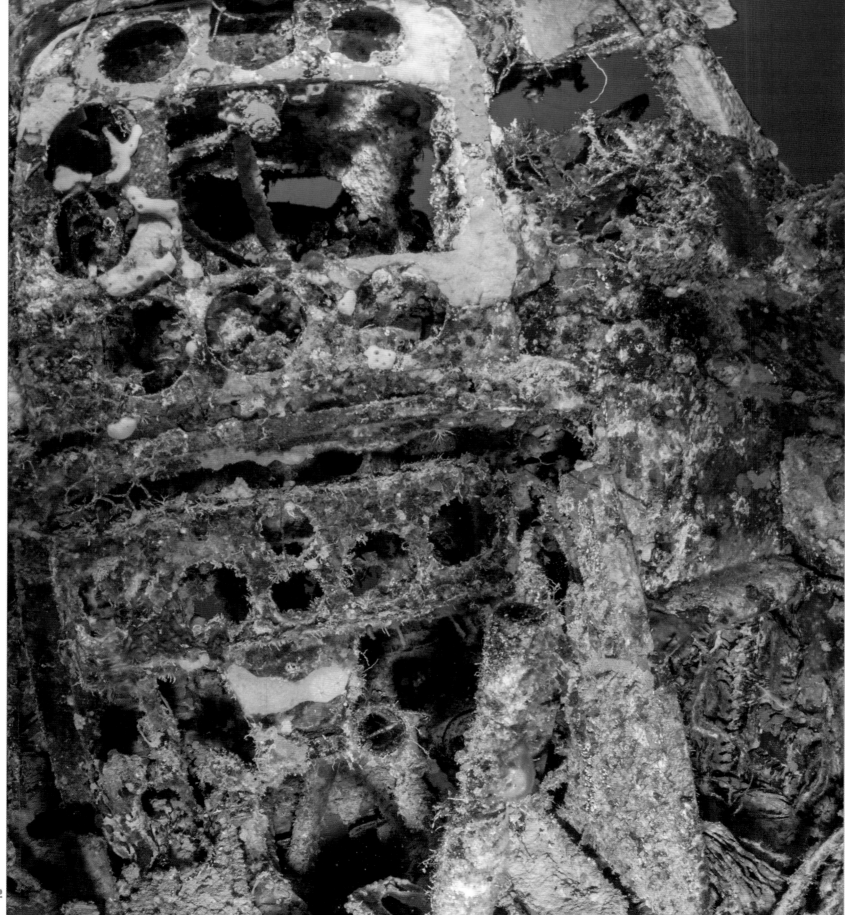

Three design features of the Dauntless make the aircraft instantly recognizable. It has a long and impressive so-called greenhouse canopy, which covers a cockpit accommodating a crew of two, the pilot and a rear-facing defensive gunner. It has round-tipped, upwardly canted gull wings and its perforated dive flaps, which span both wings, crossing under the fuselage, mark the plane as a dive bomber. In a steep dive, these flaps were deployed simultaneously upward and downward from the wing's trailing edge to hold the SBD at a constant airspeed of 250 knots (288 mph). The perforations, each three inches in diameter, piercing the flaps promoted airflow that stabilized the plane even in the steepest of dives.

The Dauntless was a pioneer of purpose-built dive bomber design, but by the time the aircraft was put into combat service, the days of dive bombing as a tactic were numbered. Early in the Pacific air war, munitions were not particularly sophisticated. The only reliable way to get a bomb on

Left: Inside the cockpit   Above: Diver explore an SBD

103

a target as small and elusive as a ship in motion was to drop the ordnance from a very low altitude. Doing this was the sole function of the naval dive bomber. The development of more accurate munitions later in the war sent dive bombing and dive bombers into decline. These innovative munitions included the High Velocity Aircraft Rocket (HVAR) with its twenty-four-pound warhead, improved aerial torpedoes, and new "skip bombing" techniques, which, like a kid skipping a stone, skipped specially designed bombs with time-delay fuses across the water and into the targeted ship.

The Dauntless was designed to deliver its bombs with great precision. It could carry a pair of 100-pound bombs on outer wing pilings as well as heavier bombs—250-pound, 500-pound, 1,000-pound—from a fork-shaped "bomb-displacing gear" located along the airplane's centerline. This ingenious device swung the large bomb downward so that, even in a steep dive, it would clear the propeller when released. The pilot used a telescopic sight mounted inside the cockpit to aim all of his bombs. Yet all this ingenuity was doomed to obsolescence. The Dauntless and its successor, the Helldiver, were the last of an exciting breed of combat aircraft.

●

It is a testament to the Dauntless that it nevertheless survived as a combatant to the very end of the war, even after the day of the dive bomber had ended. The U.S. Army Air Forces thought that the Navy SBD could be adapted for close-air support (CAS) needs: dive bombing tactical targets in coordination with ground missions. For the Army, Douglas produced the Dauntless as the A-24 Banshee dive bomber. The first of these aircraft entered service in March 1941, but never really caught on.

Strangely enough, the most numerously produced U.S. Navy version, the SBD-5, came out well after the Dauntless had been supplanted by the Helldiver. The dash-5 version had increased ammunition-carrying capacity, an illuminated bombsight, and a more powerful engine. Of 5,935 SBDs produced during World War II, 3,640 were SBD-5s. They took part in raids against the Japanese garrison on Wake Island in October 1943 and against the Japanese fleet anchored at Truk (Chuuk) lagoon in February 1944 (Operation Hailstone). Dash-5 SBDs even fought north of the Arctic Circle, in the Atlantic, on October 4, 1943, in

Operation Leader, an attack on German shipping in Bodo Harbor, Norway. But the SBD-5s flew their last major aircraft carrier operation on June 20, 1944, in an attack during the Battle of the Philippine Sea.

While the SBD-5s continued to operate in land-based USMC squadrons through V-J Day (September 2, 1945), the final Dauntless iteration, SBD-6, was produced in a quantity of just 450 before production was halted. Few of these variants were shipped overseas and none saw combat service. Slow but deadly, the Dauntless ended the war as holder of the Allied record for volume of Japanese shipping sunk in the Pacific. As grateful SBD crews added, it also held the record for the lowest loss ratio of any U.S. Navy carrier-based aircraft in World War II.

SBD planes dot the landscape of the Airplane Graveyard and it's hard to do a dive and not see at least one, or five, or more. It is by far the most numerous type of plane in the graveyard and as a rough estimate there are probably around 100 Douglas Dauntlesses scattered on the bottom. Many are found perfectly upright in the sand, but often nose down as well. Some have their wings removed (which are seen elsewhere throughout the area) but others have wings intact. Most propellers have been removed and sit in the cockpit, or are scattered nearby in the sand. One can tell how important this plane was in the WWII Pacific Theater just by how many were left on Kwajalein at the end of the war.

SBDs fly over the USS Enterprise. (Public Domain)

Bannerfish inside an SBD

Part of the interior of a PBJ

CHAPTER 5
MITCHELL: THE TEN THOUSAND

North American PBJ-1 Mitchell Medium Bomber

Crew: 5

Length: 52 ft 11 in (m)

Wingspan: 67 ft (m)

Height: 15 ft 9 in (m)

Empty weight: 19,975 lb (kg)

Loaded weight: 33,500-36.074 lb (kg)

Powerplant: 2 × Wright 2600-13 engines, 1,700 hp at takeoff (1,267 kW) each

Maximum speed: 275 mph (knots, km/h)

Cruise speed: 230 mph (knots, km/h)

Range: 1,350 mi (nmi, km)

Service ceiling: 24,200 ft (7,378 m)

Guns: 16 × 0.50 in (12.7 mm) machine guns

Bombload: 3,200 lb (kg) of bombs or 2000 lb (kg) aerial torpedoes

(Public Domain)

United States Marines have always been improvisers. They were experts at examining whatever came their way and seizing opportunity when they saw it. The Mitchell Medium bomber, best known by its U.S. Army Air Forces designation as the B-25 (its most numerous iteration was the B-25H), was enormously successful. Unsurprisingly, it was produced in very large quantity, nearly ten thousand (9,816) built in all. North American aviation pushed its assembly lines to the limit, and in 1943's frenzy of production ended up turning out more of the planes than the Air Corps could use. About 800 were offered to the Navy. That service branch has a history with the B-25, of course. On April 18, 1942, USAAF lieutenant colonel (later general) James H. "Jimmy" Doolittle led a flight of sixteen Mitchell's off the deck of USS *Hornet* in a spectacular raid against Tokyo and other targets in Japan. At this point so early in the Pacific war, the United States was hardly in a strategic position to stage an air raid against the Japanese mainland. That Doolittle nevertheless did precisely this, achieving the impossible by launching sixteen medium bombers from a carrier deck, made the raid a success far beyond the minor physical damage it inflicted on Japan. It was a tremendous propaganda coup and an Allied morale lifter.

Yet the Navy recognized that it needed carrier aircraft capable of performing more than just propaganda and morale missions. Just because it was *possible* to fly a B-25 off a carrier did not mean it was a good idea to do so. The plane was

A shark swims over a PBJ-1 Mitchell

simply too big and too heavy to be of sustained practical use in this way. The Navy passed on the offer of the 800—though it would later use a few Mitchells for land-based antisubmarine patrols. Accustomed to taking unwanted hand-me-down equipment from the Army and the Navy, the Marines decided that they had need for a medium bomber. Although the B-25 was too much plane to routinely launch from a carrier deck, it was just right for small landing fields scratched out of jungles in remote Pacific island outposts. The aircraft were well-suited to anti-shipping missions and close air support (CAS) for Marine ground and amphibious operations, especially on landings and beachheads. It could also be used for day and night "heckling," tactical hit-and-run raids on enemy positions.

Initially, the Marines took fifty B-25Cs and 152 B-25Ds from the USAAF by way of the Navy—though they did not accept them from the factory quite "as-is." To begin with, while they retained the name Mitchell—which honored William Lendrum "Billy" Mitchell, the U.S. Army general who was one of the greatest and most courageous pioneers of American military aviation—they changed the designation to "PBJ." It did not signify "peanut butter and jelly," but Patrol Bomber; the J was U.S. Navy and Marine Corps alpha-code for the manufacturer, North American Aviation.

The dash-1 appended to it, PBJ-1, indicated the initial (and only) major modifications the Marines made to the Army version of the aircraft. Marine commanders well knew that Marine aviators would use the bomber unconventionally. For one thing, they would usually fly at low altitude, whether attacking ships or providing CAS. This meant that there was little need for the bombardier position in the Plexiglas nose. The Marines therefore replaced it with a solid nose and armed this position with as many as eight .50 caliber machine guns. In some versions, a single 75 mm cannon was placed here. Both weapons were highly useful for heckling raids and for CAS.

The first Mitchell-equipped squadron was VMB-413, which was established at Cherry Point, North Carolina in March 1943. Six more squadrons saw action in the Pacific theater before the end of the war: VMB-423, VMB-433, VMB-443, VMB-611, VMB-612, and VMB-613. Collectively, these squadrons lost 173 men and forty-five PBJ-1s during the Pacific campaign. It was a sacrifice that contributed to Pacific victory, yet received very little notice

Coral growth on a tail section

from journalists or historians. Today, all but a few military historians and the most avid and dedicated Pacific war buffs even know that Leathernecks flew this warbird.

The first operational squadron, VMB-413, was nicknamed the Flying Nightmares. Under the command of Lieutenant Colonel Andrew B. Galatian Jr., it began operations from Stirling Island in the Treasury Islands Group a few miles south of Bougainville in the Solomons. Galatian's main assignment was to heckle Japanese positions and installations at Kavieng on New Ireland Island, off the New Guinea coast, and Rabaul on New Britain, largest island in the Bismarck Archipelago of what is today Papua New Guinea. If they were to be effective, these missions had to be flown when the enemy least expected them, which required flying even in adverse weather. The Japanese met the incoming bombers with anti-aircraft fire and fighter planes. Losses were very heavy in the first two months of operation, VMB-413 losing five Mitchells and the lives of twenty-seven men. When Galatian met with his pilots to discuss suspending these exceptionally hazardous missions, Captain Robert Millington spoke up for them: "Sir, we are Marines, and we don't quit!"

The mission continued, taking a heavy toll on men and machines. VMB-413 was relieved by VMB-423 for R&R (rest and rehabilitation) on May 15, 1944. It returned to combat in July. In the meantime, Lieutenant Colonel John L. Winston led VMB-423 in combat. On May 27, one of his bombers dropped a sixty-five-foot-long scroll on Rabaul, a township in the East New Britain province of New Guinea, which was a major Japanese base throughout much of the Pacific war. The scroll, signed by 35,000 Oklahoma schoolchildren who had collected money to purchase enough war bonds to buy a new B-25, accompanied a salvo of bombs designed to crater Rabaul's runways.

In June, VMB-423 moved to Green Island, about sixty miles east of New Ireland and was joined in July by VMB-433 under the command of Major John G. Adams. At this time, VMB-413 returned to action at Munda, on New Georgia Island. The "Flying Nightmares" made their first daylight bombing raid on July 29, hitting Japanese supply depots. As was typical, bombs were released at an altitude of only 150 feet. Sipasai Island was hit hard, and the PBJ crews used their nose-mounted machine guns to strafe a small Japanese auxiliary vessel nearby.

Later in the summer, PBJ squadrons were moved to Emirau, 250 miles south of Rabaul and 600 miles south of Truk (Chuuk). At this time, Lieutenant Colonel Dwight M. Guillotte's VMB-443 squadron arrived, and, with the other two squadrons, repeatedly bombed targets in the Bismarck Archipelago. In the fall, an advance element of VMB-611 arrived, commanded by Lieutenant Colonel George A. Sarles. The augmented bombing force now made daily strikes against the Japanese at Kavieng and Rabaul.

In 1945, the commanding general of First Marine Aircraft Wing, Major General Ralph J. Mitchell, persuaded theater commanders to deploy some of his PBJ squadrons in the Philippine campaign. Marine bombers began combat operations there in March, and, for the next four months, they relentlessly attacked Japanese positions in Mindanao, thereby staking their claim on a small but significant role in the most extensive amphibious campaign of the Pacific war.

In addition to hitting Mindanao in the southern Philippines, the Marine PBJs flew long-range patrols over Mindoro, off the southwest coast of Luzon, and as far as Borneo. In addition to heckling raids and tactical bombing, especially at night, the PBJs extensively supported American ground missions throughout the Philippines. It was in this period that Marine aviators brought CAS to a high level of effectiveness, which substantially reduced casualties among U.S. soldiers and Marines on the ground.

The toll on the Marine aviators and their aircraft was heavy in the Philippines. Nevertheless, during April and May, the men of VMB-611 flew 173 sorties and dropped approximately 245 tons of bombs, fired 800 rockets, and disgorged untold quantities of machine-gun rounds. Whatever it cost the Marines, it cost the enemy far more in disrupted troop movements, loss of supplies, destruction of airfields and artillery, and loss of vehicles, not to mention the erosion of Japanese morale. In July, VMB-611 combined night heckling runs with leaflet-drops, blanketing surviving—and starving—Japanese troops with messages urging their surrender.

While a large portion of the Marine PBJ force was dedicated to operations in the Philippines during the final months of the war, other squadrons continued to pound Rabaul. The squadrons were used not only for CAS and other ground-bombing operations, but also against ships. In the fall of 1944, Marine aviators attacked and sank submarines and surface vessels—mostly freighters—near the Bonin Islands, some 620 miles due south of Tokyo. These operations continued into the early months of 1945 and were especially effective against commercial shipping.

In December 1944, the last PBJ squadron to arrive in the Pacific Theater, VMB-613, commanded by Major George W. Nevils, landed on Kwajalein Island. It operated from here beginning on December 23, attacking island strongholds throughout the Marshall group, concentrating on those that had been bypassed for naval bombardment and ground invasion in Admiral Nimitz's and General MacArthur's "island-hopping" campaign. At the same time, the squadron also attacked enemy ships. Its most notable mission was a raid against Pohnpei Island in the Caroline group on February 6, 1945. The raid was highly effective, despite encountering heavy anti-aircraft fire. Two PBJs were badly hit. In one, the navigator was killed, but the aircraft limped home. As for the other, which had been the last plane over the target, a direct flak hit had badly damaged its right wing. Incredibly, the crew made it to the Kwaj runway, but the damaged wing collapsed during landing and the aircraft crashed at the runway's end, exploding on impact with the loss of the entire crew.

Some PBJs had a search radar fitted on the starboard wingtip

A PBJ with both engines having fallen off

Left: The weight of the engines probably is what caused many to fall off directly in front of the planes. Inside the engine is now a home for marine life like coral

Above: A PBJ engine covered with coral

The Marines developed remarkable CAS and low-level bombing tactics with their PBJ-1s. As mentioned, such improvisatory innovation was and remains a USMC trademark. But the Marine aircrew themselves also gave credit to the great versatility of the bomber that had been handed down to them.

North American began its design work on what would become the B-25 Mitchell in response to specifications issued by the Air Corps in March 1938, calling for a generation of medium bombers with a payload of 1,200 pounds (540 kg) and a range of 1,200 miles (1,900 km) capable of cruising in excess of 200 miles per hour (320 km/h). Company engineers designed the NA-40, which was based on an experimental bomber, the XB-21, prototyped in 1936. The Army had accepted this very iteration, only to cancel the order due to some design flaws. Nevertheless, North American persevered, learned from the reported deficiencies, and had the NA-40 in the air by late January 1939. When it became apparent that the aircraft needed more power, new 1,600-horsepower Wright R-2600 "Twin Cyclone" radial engines were installed in March 1939. The NA-40B was flown against competitors from Douglas, Stearman, and Martin. It lost out to Martin.

In March 1939, the Air Corps published a new medium bomber specification. This one called for a payload of 2,400 pounds (1,100 kg) at a range of 1,200 miles (1,900 km) cruising at 300 miles per hour. North American responded by developing the NA-40B design to produce the NA-62, which, in September 1939, won an Army order, despite falling short of the 300 mile-per-hour spec. As the B-25 Mitchell, it would go into production alongside its competitor, the Martin B-26 Marauder, which, acquiring a reputation for being hard to fly (pilots called it "The Widowmaker"), was produced in about half the number (5,288) as the B-25.

North American aggressively continued to improve the B-25's design throughout production, most visibly by transforming the original flat wings into slightly bent gull wings to add flight stability. The size of the tail fins was also increased while their inward slant was decreased. Armaments were upgraded throughout production, and the aircraft became an increasingly versatile platform, usable not only as a conventional medium bomber, but as a very able strafer and a gunship that could concentrate fire on a very small area of ground.

The need for such versatility in the bomber was of a piece with the Marines' recognition of the value of their own versatility as a combat force. The roles of single-engine fighter aircraft on the one hand and heavy, four-engine bombers on the other were clear-cut. But World War II—truly a world war, fought across a far-flung geography, much of it in the Pacific, remote from major centers of population—demanded that medium bombers be capable of playing multiple roles. Jimmy Doolittle proved that the B-25 could be taught to fly off of an aircraft carrier. Shortly thereafter, the Marines proved that Doolittle's feat was just the beginning. As the PBJ-1, the Mitchell could be taught to handle virtually any mission from 10,000 feet down to 150. An unplanned—almost accidental—combination, Marine aviators flying the Mitchell bomber proved to be a war-winning match.

The PBJ-1 Mitchells are one of the favorite planes in the graveyard for divers. Large in size, they are really exciting to dive, as their expanse makes a diver feel small. Eleven PBJs were documented to have been dumped off Roi-Namur in October 1945, and all eleven have GPS coordinates for divers to easily find and visit them. Ten of eleven sit upright in the sand and the eleventh, which is upside down, is unique among the others because you can see the bottom of the plane, including open bomb doors. They are also still very much intact. Some of the engines have fallen off into the sand, probably due to their weight, but several are still attached. Diving among them is a truly unique experience.

Left: Open bomb doors on the upside down PBJ

THE 11 PBJ-1 MITCHELLS IN THE AIRPLANE GRAVEYARD

(Public Domain)

CHAPTER 6
AVENGERS AMONG OTHERS

In 1921, three years after he had compiled a spectacular record leading breakthrough large-scale aerial bombing missions in World War I, U.S. Army Brigadier General William L. "Billy" Mitchell staged four dramatic demonstrations of air power at sea. These were the culmination of his theory that aircraft were destined to become a major—if not the leading—combat weapon in future wars. He moved for the creation of a U.S. Air Force independent of both the Army and the Navy. Predictably, these services pushed back—hard. And when Mitchell predicted that aircraft launched from what he called "floating bases" (the term *aircraft carrier* did not yet exist) would make battleships and other surface vessels obsolete, Navy brass were furious. Mitchell believed that the millions of dollars earmarked for the construction of a new generation of "dreadnought" battleships, a weapon rooted in the past, would take precious funds away from the development of military aviation, the true weapon of the future.

Mitchell persuaded Secretary of the Navy Josephus Daniels and Secretary of War Newton Baker to approve a series of joint Army-Navy tests, "Project B," which used surplus and captured ships as targets for aerial bombing demonstrations. On June 21, July 13, and July 18, the aircrews and aircraft of Mitchell's 1st Provisional Air Brigade flying out of Langley Field in Hampton, Virginia in concert with Navy aircraft, dropped bombs to sink a German destroyer and a German light cruiser. On July 21, Army, Navy, and Marine aircraft targeted the German battleship Ostfriesland, displacing some 23,000 tons and mounting a total of forty-six guns, including a dozen twelve-inchers.

The aircraft made short work of the German dreadnought and provoked a storm of controversy that led to Mitchell's court martial for insubordination in 1925 but nevertheless opened the way to the development of American naval aviation. At the time, three technologies for the aerial bombardment of ships were available. One was conventional bombing, which, under combat conditions, was often inaccurate. The second was dive bombing, which required aircraft, such as the Curtiss SB2C Helldiver and the Douglas SBD Dauntless, specially designed and engineered to make steep high-speed dives on ships, so that bombs could be dropped at very low altitudes to increase accuracy. The third technology involved replacing bombs with torpedoes.

World War I had amply proved the ship- or submarine-launched torpedo to be a highly effective ship-killing munition. Torpedoes were much longer, bulkier, and heavier than conventional aerial bombs because they contained not only an explosive warhead but a self-contained propulsion system and an inertial guidance system to keep them running straight and level. They were also engineered to be seaworthy. The combination of all these features makes designing a torpedo bomber very difficult. The aircraft must be sufficiently tough and powerful to carry a heavy payload practically equivalent to a miniature submarine. At the same time, it must be a single-engine aircraft small enough to be launched from an aircraft carrier and sufficiently fast and agile enough to avoid becoming a sitting duck in the air.

The first truly practical torpedo bomber was the Douglas TBD Devastator, which the Navy ordered in 1934. It first flew in 1935, and it was introduced into the U.S. fleet years prior to World War II in the summer of 1937. In the year of its introduction, it was certainly the U.S. Navy's most advanced aircraft and, in fact, represented the cutting-edge of naval aviation worldwide. That technological supremacy did not last long, however, and the performance of the TBD at the Battle of Midway (June 4-7, 1942) proved its fatal obsolescence. Forty-one Devastators were launched, not one scored a hit on a Japanese ship, and only a half-dozen survived to return to their carriers. After the battle, the Douglas TBD was essentially retired from active service. The Devastator had been devastated.

GRUMMAN TBF AVENGER

Crew: 3

Length: 40 ft 11.5 in (12.48 m)

Wingspan: 54 ft 2 in (16.51 m)

Height: 15 ft 5 in (4.70 m)

Empty weight: 10,545 lb (4,783 kg)

Loaded weight: 17,893 lb (8,115 kg)

Powerplant: 1 × Wright R-2600-20 Twin Cyclone radial engine, 1,900 hp (1,420 kW)

Maximum speed: 275 mph (239 knots, 442 km/h)

Range: 1,000 mi (869 nmi, 1,610 km)

Service ceiling: 30,100 ft (9,170 m)

Rate of climb: 2,060 ft/min (10.5 m/s)

Guns: 1 × 0.30 in (7.62 mm) nose-mounted M1919 Browning machine gun or 2 × 0.50 in (12.7 mm) wing-mounted M2 Browning machine guns

1 × 0.50 in (12.7 mm) dorsal-mounted M2 Browning machine gun

1 × 0.30 in (7.62 mm) ventral-mounted M1919 Browning machine gun

Rockets: up to 8 eight × 3.5 in forward-firing aircraft rockets, 5 in forward firing aircraft rockets or high-velocity aerial rockets

Bombload/torpedo: 2,000 lb (907 kg) of bombs or

1 × 2,000 lb (907 kg) Mark 13 torpedo

Avenger on the USS Enterprise (Public Domain)

The Grumman TBF Avenger was designed expressly to replace the Douglas TBD Devastator. The first of two prototypes flew on August 7, 1941. Both of these XTBF-1s crashed, but production went ahead anyway, and the aircraft was introduced into service in 1942. It was the heaviest single-engine aircraft any country flew in World War II, and its weight caused some concern over the ability of carrier flight decks to support it, especially on landing. Because of its enormous fifty-four-foot wingspan, Grumman patented the "Sto-Wing," a compound-angle wing-folding system in which the wings were not simply folded straight up for storage, but twisted and folded back along the fuselage.

The TBF carried a crew of three seated in tandem: a pilot, ventral gunner (who doubled as a radioman and navigator), and a gunner in a rear-facing ball turret behind the long "greenhouse" cockpit canopy. Early models had a single .30 in machine gun mounted in the nose, and later models instead mounted two .50 in machine guns in the wings. In both versions, these were operated by the pilot. The ventral gunner operated a .30 in machine gun that was mounted on the belly of the aircraft to defend against fighters approaching from below. The turret gunner had a .50 in machine gun that fired from his electrically operated turret. In contrast to the TBD Devastator, which carried its torpedo externally, on the aircraft's belly, the TBF had a massive bomb bay, which accommodated the torpedo, one 2,000-pound bomb, or as many as four 500-pound bombs.

●

The Avenger made its public debut in a ceremony Grumman staged at the opening of a new manufacturing

The upright Avenger in the Airplane Graveyard sits in the sand with semi-folded wings, covered by a cloud of fish.

plant. That was on the afternoon of December 7, 1941. Word of the Pearl Harbor attack reached the plant immediately after the unveiling. The visitors were ushered off-site, and the brand-new factory was heavily guarded against feared sabotage. The first 100 plus aircraft produced in that plant were shipped off to the Navy in June 1942. They arrived in Pearl Harbor just hours after the three fleet carriers had departed, bound for the fateful Battle of Midway. The bad timing meant that most of the new Grummans did not participate in this turning-point battle—though six did arrive at Midway in time to fight. Five were shot out of the sky. The sixth limped back to the USS *Hornet* badly banged up. One gunner

had been killed and the other wounded, along with the pilot. Yet the Navy did not count this as a defeat. The torpedo bombers—both the badly outclassed Devastators and the six Avengers—had served to lure away Japanese carrier-launched combat patrols, which gave the SBD Dauntless dive bombers the cover they needed to sink all four Japanese carriers at Midway.

The Avengers went on to compile a much more unambiguously successful record in the Pacific after Midway. Surely, this was partly due to the design and performance of the aircraft, a great advance over the Devastator, but its subsequent success also reflected the greater experience of its veteran pilots and the better training of newbies, such

The fifty-four-foot wingspan of the Avenger had a compound-angle wing-folding system where they twisted back along the fuselage called "Sto-Wing."

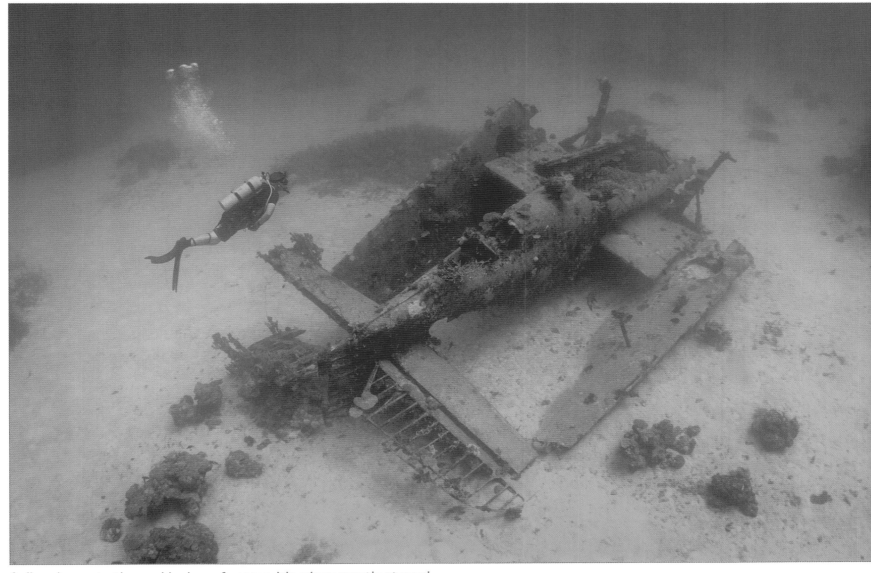

A diver inspects the upside down Avenger, it's wings mostly stowed.

as future-President George H. W. Bush. Commissioned in June 1943, Bush was the youngest aviator in the U.S. Navy at the time. He was shot down in his Avenger, flying from the escort carrier *San Jacinto*, on September 2, 1944, over Chichi Jima Island. He managed to release his bombs and hit his assigned target before bailing out into the Pacific. Although both of his gunners died, he was picked up by the submarine Finback, and he was later decorated with the Distinguished Flying Cross (Another famous figure associated with the Avenger was the actor Paul Newman. In World War II, the nineteen-year-old aspired to be a naval aviator but was disqualified by color blindness and was assigned instead as a turret gunner).

As for the Avengers, they fought with great distinction in the Eastern Solomons on August 24, 1942. A total of twenty-four launched from the carriers *Saratoga* and *Enterprise* sank the Japanese light carrier *Ryūjō* and shot down a Japanese dive bomber. Seven Avengers were lost in the action. In November 1942, a combination of USMC and Navy Avengers sank the battleship *Hiei* (forty-four guns, 36,600 tons displacement) in the Naval Battle of Guadalcanal.

Relatively early in production—before a thousand had been built—the TBF-1C variant was introduced with greater fuel capacity thanks to bigger internal tanks and drop tanks mounted under the wings. This doubled the plane's original range to 2,000 miles. In 1943, Grumman responded to increased orders for the new F6F Hellcat fighter by transferring production of the Avenger to the Eastern Aircraft Division of General Motors. This generation of Avengers were called TBMs—*M* being the alpha code for GM-produced aircraft, *F* signifying Grumman. A new iteration, the TBM-3, began rolling off GM assembly lines in mid-1944, featuring a more powerful engine and improved wing hardpoints to accommodate larger drop tanks as well as rockets. Of the 9,839 Avengers produced, some 4,600 were the TBM-3 variant.

As a torpedo bomber, the Avenger was designed to sink surface ships, but it proved a prolific slayer of submarines as well, killing some thirty, both in the Pacific and the Atlantic. The biggest prizes claimed by Avengers were the two Japanese *Yamoto*-class super battleships, *Musashi* and *Yamato*. These vessels were the heaviest and most formidably armed battleships ever constructed, each displacing nearly 73,000 tons and armed with nine 18.1-inch guns and fifty-two of lesser caliber. *Musashi* was sunk at the Battle of Leyte Gulf on October 24, 1944, and *Yamoto* was sent to the bottom in Operation Ten-Go during the Okinawa Campaign on April 7, 1945.

Not long after the war, the Avenger entered history for a more mysterious reason. On December 5, 1945, a training flight of five of the aircraft—Flight 19—disappeared while flying within the Bermuda Triangle. This loss is the foundation of the legends surrounding the area of the Atlantic bounded on the west by the tip of Florida, the southeast by Puerto Rico, and the northeast by Bermuda.

TBF Avengers flying in formation. (Public Domain)

The upside down Avenger.

There are only two Avengers known to be in the graveyard and they both show the unique "Sto-Wing" folding characteristics. One Avenger is completely upside down with the wings folded, the other sits upright and you can see the wings semi-folded. The upright Avenger is my favorite plane in the graveyard. It sits in the sand very close to the barrier reef, making it shallower than most of the planes. I also just love the way the Avenger looks, in my mind it's the plane that comes to mind when I imagine WWII.

VOUGHT F4U CORSAIR

Crew: 1

Length: 33 ft 8 in (10.26 m)

Wingspan: 41 ft 0 in (12.50 m)

Height: 14 ft 9 in (4.50 m)

Empty weight: 9,205 lb (4,175 kg)

Powerplant: 1 × Pratt & Whitney R-2800-18W radial engine, 2,380 hp (1,770 kW)

Maximum speed: 446 mph (718 km/h; 388 knots)

Range: 1,005 mi (1,617 km; 873 nmi)

Combat range: 328 mi (528 km; 285 nmi)

Service ceiling: 41,500 ft (12,600 m)

Rate of climb: 4,360 ft/min (22.1 m/s)

Guns: 6 × 0.50 in (12.7 mm) M2 Browning machine guns or

4 × 0.79 in (20 mm) AN/M3 cannon

Rockets/bombs: 8 × 5 in (12.7 cm) high velocity aircraft rockets and/or up to

4,000 pounds (1,800 kg) of bombs

One of the most successful fighter designs of World War II, the Vought F4U Corsair continued to be produced well beyond the end of the war, manufactured from 1942 to 1953. By the time production ended, 12,571 had been delivered. The navy of Honduras was still flying the aircraft as late as 1979. The United States Navy and Marine Corps flew the F4U in World War II as well as the Korean War. World War II demand for the aircraft was so heavy that Corsair had to share production with Brewster Aeronautical Corporation and the Goodyear Company.

Although the Corsair was designed for carrier flight, it became more closely associated with the U.S. Marines, who flew it from Pacific island land bases over a wide area of the vast theater in World War II. Indeed, the Marines were the first to fly the Corsairs in combat, operating them from land bases before the aircraft had received its final certification for carrier flight. Marine pilots received 965 FG-1A models, which had been built for land use, without their hydraulic wing-folding mechanisms. Later, after the carrier-ready Corsairs were being produced, Marine mechanics removed the folding mechanisms in the field, along with catapult hooks and arresting hooks. Shedding these last two items saved fliers forty-eight pounds.

Whether flown by Navy or Marine aviators, the Corsair earned a reputation as the most formidable American fighter plane of World War II. That was the judgment of the Japanese aviators who had the misfortune of going up against it in combat.

•

The Corsair began life in response to a February 1938 Navy request for proposals for a single-engine fighter capable of the "maximum obtainable speed" and with a range of 1,000 miles. The Navy wanted it armed with four guns—or three with high ammunition capacity—and (what seems strange now) the ability to carry anti-aircraft bombs in the wing. The idea was that the Corsairs could release these small munitions above flying enemy formations. This impractical tactic was never actually employed.

Vought won a contract in June 1938 to produce a prototype, XF4U-1, which was very quickly approved for production for the Navy. It had the biggest, most powerful engine, the largest propeller, and the largest wing on any naval fighter to that date. As for the "maximum" speed spec, the XF4U-1 became the first U.S. single-engine fighter to exceed 400 miles per hour on October 1, 1940. In fact, some aspects of F4U performance exceeded the ability of the airframe to handle their effects. In a power dive, the aircraft reached 550 miles per hour, but suffered control-surface damage and, in one case, engine failure. Maneuvers at very high speeds also caused stability problems. Production was delayed until the kinks were worked out. In April 1941, the Navy contracted for 584 Corsairs. The first production F4U-1 flew on June 24, 1942, and the aircraft were introduced into service on December 28 of that year.

For the first time the Navy was flying a fighter that's performance was demonstrably superior to its contemporaries, both friendly and enemy. This made it quite a handful for inexperienced pilots. Its small "birdcage" cockpit canopy, set *behind* the trailing edge of the wing to accommodate the huge Pratt & Whitney R-2800-18W engine, reduced visibility when taxiing and landing. On land, a member of the ground crew would often perch on the leading edge of the wing to signal the pilot as he taxied into position for take-off. The engine's awesome torque threatened to get many a pilot in trouble, and the Corsair was dubbed the "bent-wing widow maker."

The Corsair's long "hose nose" made the plane difficult for some pilots to land on carrier decks, but the Marines found the improvement in performance over the Grumman F4F Wildcat so dramatic that they quickly embraced the fighter, which they flew beginning in February 1943 from bases in Guadalcanal and, later, from other bases in the Solomons. The Marines' maiden battle with the aircraft was not auspicious, however. On February 14, Corsairs of VMF-124 assisted U.S. Army Air Force P-40s and P-38s in escorting a large formation of four-engine B-24 Liberators on a bombing raid against a Japanese air base at Kahili, near Buin, Bougainville in what is today Papua New Guinea. Japanese Zero fighters attacked, shooting down four P-38s, two P-40s, two Corsairs, and a pair of Liberators. Four Zeros were destroyed, including one in a midair collision with a Corsair.

The Marines soon lived down this tragic humiliation, which was called the "St. Valentine's Day Massacre." Within a few months, Marine Corps pilots were consistently winning against their Japanese opponents.

Corsairs in flight. (Public Domain)

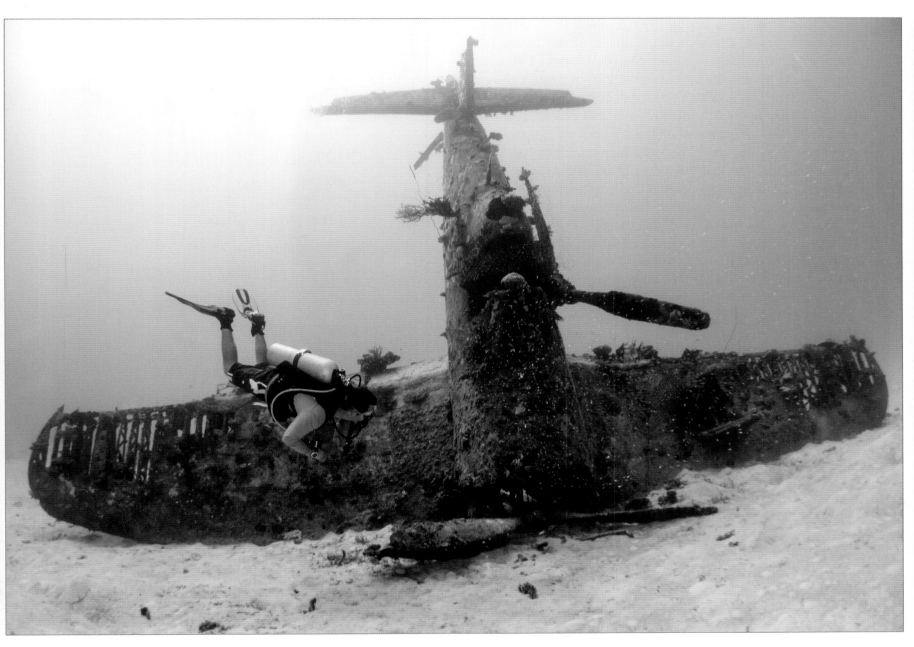

Left: Lionfish on the Corsair
Above: Diver on the Corsair

•

The genealogy of the F4F may be traced to the Grumman FF, a biplane Navy fighter—the first carrier plane to boast retractable landing gear—prototyped in 1931 and introduced into the fleet in 1933. Just 116 were built before Grumman went on to design the F2F and F3F, still biplane designs, but with the compact fuselage of the future F4F monoplane. Grumman was spurred to develop the F4F when the U.S. Navy turned away from the F3F in a move toward the Brewster F2A-1, which was a monoplane. The Navy was quickly disappointed in the Brewster and placed a backup order with Grumman based on the XF4F-1, an experimental prototype that, like the F3F, was a biplane. Grumman engineers soon realized that this new biplane would not outperform the Brewster monoplane. Grumman therefore decided to retain the XF4F-1 fuselage, but redesign the rest of the aircraft as a monoplane. With that, the XF4F-2 was born.

In flight tests, the Grumman, even as a monoplane, was not as agile as the Brewster Buffalo, though it was a bit faster. Realizing that it could not win a Navy contract with a partial redesign, Grumman produced the XF4F-3, which incorporated not only a new wing design, but a revised tail and mounted a supercharged version of the Pratt & Whitney R-1830 Twin Wasp radial engine. The aircraft was a breakthrough, and the Navy placed an order for the F4F-3. Delivery came in February 1940, and it was introduced into the fleet that December. A quantity ordered by France was diverted to the British Royal Navy when the French capitulated to the Germans at the end of the Battle of France (June 25, 1940). The Brits called it the "Martlet." The Americans preferred "Wildcat."

The surprisingly impressive war record of the Wildcat, already obsolescent by the time the United States entered the war in December 1941, was the result of two things: the superior ruggedness of the Grumman aircraft, which absorbed remarkable punishment, and the superior tactics of American aviators. U.S. Navy commander John Smith "Jimmy" Thach analyzed encounters between Japanese Zeroes and Navy Wildcats. He concluded that the Wildcat pilots could compensate for their lesser speed against the Zeroes through a coordinated defensive maneuver that became known as the "Thach Weave." Two or more Wildcats would fly regularly intersecting paths with one another, so that any Zero chasing one of them would become vulnerable to counterattack by the other. The combination of durability and tactics made the bantamweight Wildcat a formidable combatant, and the F4F was produced in a quantity of 7,885.

The graveyard has an area that seems to be almost littered with Wildcats. As a diver swims in one direction there are scattered fuselages lying all around. Some have wings folded, some are missing the wings, or the wings are laying about in between other airplane parts. These planes generally have a lot of marine growth on them and there is a lot of coral in the area, so they blend in and sometimes it's difficult to make out if it's a plane part or a coral head.

CURTISS SB2C HELLDIVER

Crew: 2

Length: 36 ft 8 in (11.18 m)

Wingspan: 49 ft 9 in (15.17 m)

Height: 13 ft 2 in (4.01 m)

Empty weight: 10,547 lb (4,794 kg)

Loaded weight: 16,616 lb (7,553 kg)

Powerplant: 1 × Wright R-2600-20 Twin Cyclone radial engine, 1,900 hp (1,417 kW)

Maximum speed: 295 mph (257 knots, 475 km/h) at 16,700 ft (5,090 m)

Range: 1,165 mi (1,013 nmi, 1,876 km)

Service ceiling: 29,100 ft (8,870 m)

Rate of climb: 1,800 ft/min (9.1 m/s)

Guns: 2 × 20 mm (.79 in) AN/M2 cannon in the wings

2 × 0.30 in (7.62 mm) AN/M2 Browning machine guns in the rear cockpit

Rockets: 8 × 5 in (12.7 cm) high-velocity aircraft rockets

Bombs/torpedo: 2,000 lb (900 kg) bombload or 1 × Mark 13-2 torpedo in the internal bay; 500 lb (225 kg) of bombs on each underwing hardpoint

Wildcats taking off from USS Enterprise. (Public Domain)

Wildcat mostly buried in the sand

Built to replace the Douglas SBD Dauntless, the Helldiver was significantly faster and more versatile (it could double as a conventional bomber and as a torpedo bomber in addition to performing as a dive bomber), but it came into service just as the demand for dive bombers was beginning to decline. The aircraft thus entered the fleet with the whiff of obsolescence. That was strike one. Strike two was its difficult handling characteristics. Pilots claimed that "SB2C" stood for "Son of a Bitch, 2nd Class."

Strike three? The airplane was ugly, a "Big-Tailed Beast" with a long nose that made for poor visibility in aircraft carrier take-off and landing. The Senate Special Committee to Investigate the National Defense Program, better known as

the Truman Committee (after its chairman, Senator—and future vice-president and president—Harry S. Truman), condemned faulty production practices and interminable delays at Curtiss, but the Navy remained determined to fix the problems. Only after Curtiss made a staggering total of 880 separate modifications was the airplane finally accepted into service in December 1942. It did not see combat until November of the following year. But, during those last two years of World War II, the SB2C racked up an impressive combat record in the Pacific Theater.

The airplanes truly came into their own in 1944 in combat over the Marianas, the Philippines (where SB2Cs participated in the sinking of the super-battleship *Musashi*),

Wildcat with folded wings

Taiwan, Iwo Jima, and Okinawa (where the aircraft partici-pated in the destruction of *Musashi*'s sister ship, the *Yamato*).

In the closing battles of the war, SB2Cs attacked the Ryukyu Islands and the Japanese home island of Honshu, focusing mainly on cratering Japanese airfields and dis-rupting communications and shipping. Although the U.S. Marines took delivery of 410 Helldivers from the U.S. Army (which called the plane the A-25A Shrike), they used it exclusively for training purposes, never in combat.

Only one complete Helldiver resides in the graveyard and other than a partially cracked wing, it is in great con-dition. At least one other set of Helldiver wings have been found, but their purpose as spares or perhaps a part of another complete plane is unknown.

Folded wings of a Wildcat, amidst fish and coral

Fish life inside the cockpit of a Wildcat

CURTISS C-46 COMMANDO

Crew: 4

Capacity: 40 troops or 30 stretcher patients or 15,000 lb (6,800 kg) cargo

Length: 76 ft 4 in (23.27 m)

Wingspan: 108 ft 0 in (32.91 m)

Height: 21 ft 9 in (6.62 m)

Empty weight: 30,669 lb (14,700 kg)

Loaded weight: 45,000 lb (20,412 kg)

Powerplant: 2 × Pratt & Whitney R-2800-51 two-row 18-cylinder radial engines, 2,000 hp (1,492 kW) each

Maximum speed: 270 mph (235 knots, 435 km/h)

Cruising speed: 173 mph (150 knots, 278 km/h)

Range: 3,150 mi (2,739 nmi, 5,069 km)

Service ceiling: 24,500 ft (7,468 m)

Helldivers on the USS Yorktown. (Public Domain)

More than a few World War II aircraft achieved iconic status, ranging from celebrated warbirds like the Avenger to rugged unarmed transport aircraft like the C-47. Another transport, the Curtiss C-46 Commando, fell short of C-47 both as an icon (all but historical aviation buffs would likely be unable to identify it) and in terms of production. The C-46 was produced in a quantity of 3,185 between 1940 and 1945, whereas the C-47 reached 10,174 units.

Like the C-47, the C-46 was developed from a civilian airliner predecessor. The origin of the C-47 was the DC-3, which first flew in 1935 and is *still* in passenger and cargo service in various parts of the world today—though the last aircraft were produced in 1950. While the DC-3 revolutionized commercial air travel—it was deemed the first airliner that could make a profit from flying passengers alone—it never featured a pressurized cabin. *That* was the

breakthrough Curtiss sought with its CW-20. High-altitude flight is both more economical and more comfortable than flying at levels that do not require oxygen. Yet, whereas Douglas sold its DC-3 to numerous airlines, Curtiss proved unable to gain a commitment from them. It therefore turned to the military, which ordered them primarily as unpressurized cargo planes.

The C-46 earned a degree of fame operating in the remote China-Burma-India theater (the "CBI"). It flew the infamously hazardous trans-Himalaya "Hump" route, carrying desperately needed supplies from British India to China after the Japanese had seized control of all overland and water routes. The C-46 proved to be uniquely suited to withstanding the extremes of weather, the Himalayan altitudes, and the miserable landing fields. It also could handle very heavy cargo loads. By volume, the C-46 had twice the cargo capacity of the C-47, and by weight, it could carry *three* times as much.

Helldiver

A set of Helldiver wings in a different area of the graveyard

SB2C Helldivers flying (Public Domain)

C-46. (Public Domain)

Flying "The Hump" was a U.S. Army Air Forces mission. The Marines used the C-46 in their Pacific island campaigns. Their version was designated the R5C, and it became a logistics workhorse. Marine aviators made use of every cubic inch of cargo and passenger capacity as well as the aircraft's long range to transport men and equipment over vast Pacific distances. The R5C also earned a reputation as a bird of mercy. It was used to evacuate badly wounded personnel from combat zones.

There is only one C-46 fuselage in the graveyard. It is missing its tail and its wings, although at least four wings that are likely for the C-46 have been found in other sections of the graveyard. It makes sense that the wings were removed from this plane in order to fit as many planes as possible onto the barges that dumped them. Divers can explore the massive cargo area inside the C-46 and imagine how much supplies or men could have fit within.

Left: Inside cockpit of the C-46
Above: C-46

Inside the C-46, looking towards the tail.

Douglas SBD Dauntless

AFTERWORD

For many communities, the local graveyard is a repository of memory. For the people of Kwaj, the Airplane Graveyard is a reminder that the past is very directly connected to the current state and future of Kwajalein Atoll and the Marshall Islands. The planes that rest below, mostly unknown or forgotten, mirror the situation of the island nation to which they now belong. It, too, is mostly unknown to or forgotten by the world beyond it.

Yet, what is at the bottom of the lagoon reminds us of a vast world war that engulfed even this very improbable place in the Central Pacific. This same small island country today plays a key role in United States missile defense and space studies. Few people know that Kwajalein also hosts one of the planet's four dedicated ground antennas, which are vital to the operation of the Global Positioning System (GPS) navigation system (The other three antennas are at Ascension Island in the South Atlantic, Diego Garcia in the central Indian Ocean, and Cape Canaveral in Florida).

POSTWAR

On February 6, 1944, Kwajalein was claimed by the United States, and, after being used by the U.S. as a staging area for its advance against Japan, Kwaj and the rest of the Marshall Islands were designated after the war as a United Nations Trust Territory under the United States.

World War II ended for the Marshalls, but the islands would feel the heat of the Cold War that followed. The U.S. military continued to use several islands in different atolls for nuclear testing. Sixty-seven weapons tests occurred in the postwar years, including the test of the first hydrogen bomb ("Mike") at Eniwetok Atoll in 1952. Kwajalein Atoll served as the main command center for much of the nuclear and thermonuclear testing, which began with Operation Crossroads in 1946, in which two of three planned tests occurred at Bikini Atoll, 256 miles away, to assess the impact of nuclear weapons on a target of ninety-five captured or surplus warships lined up in the lagoon. The vessels were filled with fuel, ammunition, and even live animals, so that the tests might reveal the full range of impact.

During the testing, island residents were forced to scatter to numerous locations and were unable to return until long after the tests. At last, in the 1970s they were told they could move back to Bikini. After they did, however, further analysis showed persistent widespread radioactive contamination. The United States paid damages to the islanders and paid as well for radiological cleanup. Yet compensation claims continue to be litigated today. In 1998, Congress set up a Nuclear Claims Tribunal, which paid out $45.8 million in personal injury claims until 2009, when the tribunal's funds ran out. Today, about half the valid claimants have died without having received compensation. Congress has made no moves to fund the tribunal further, and it is not likely that remaining claimants will ever see more money. In 1964 the United States began its anti-ballistic missile testing, which continues to this day. The U.S. military leases several islands, with payments going directly to the land owners.

In 1986 the Republic of the Marshall Islands (RMI) became independent under a Compact of Free Association with the United States. The Compact allows RMI nationals to legally enter, live, work, and go to school in the United States. Some do. Conversation with my RMI co-workers and other people living on Ebeye or Ennibur made it clear that going to the U.S. is a common goal. Some I talked with had already gone to the United States, lived and worked there for a time, and then returned to the islands. Others were trying to send their kids to the States. Hawaii, not surprisingly, is home to a significant RMI community, but so are some unexpected mainland states, such as Utah and Arkansas (More than 4,000 have relocated to Arkansas).

Most of the revenue that comes into the RMI is in the form of U.S. assistance or lease payments. About $1 billion in aid came between 1986 and 2001 under the Compact of Free Association. A new Compact was negotiated for 2004-2024, by which the RMI will receive $1.5 billion. There is also a jointly funded Trust Fund designed to provide an

A nuclear weapon is tested at Bikini Atoll in 1946, part of Operation Crossroads (Public Domain)

income stream to the islands after 2024, when the direct Compact aid ends. In truth, no one knows what will happen after 2024. Presumably, the United States will continue to lease the islands for both their strategic position in the Pacific and for the infrastructure of military defense that is already in place. Time will tell.

CHALLENGES OF TODAY

Despite aid, a quick walk around Ebeye or Majuro reveals extreme poverty. The islands of the RMI are at extremely low elevations and made of coral and sand. This land does not support major agriculture, and fresh water is scarce, since its only source is rain, and droughts have been plentiful. Food has also become a problem with increasing population, especially as fishery stocks have been depleted from commercial fishing and the increase of diseased fish

from pollution and runoff into lagoons. Food and sometimes fresh water are imported via cargo ships, but this comes at a cost most islanders cannot afford.

In addition to drought and scarcity of potable water, the islanders face pollution. The island's garbage often ends up in the ocean. As if that weren't enough, garbage washes up on the shores from faraway places and from offshore ships. Ebeye and Majuro are very densely populated, and raw sewage, mostly human waste, washes into the lagoon, contaminating the water as well as the fish the islanders consume. Climate change is another concern, since even a slight sea-level rise could cause the islands to disappear. Currently, land erosion and flooding from increasingly heavy rains and high tides are serious issues. On those islands the U.S. Army does not lease, people have only rudimentary housing, which is easily damaged or even washed away.

Left and Above: Trash on the beaches of Ebeye

LIVING ON KWAJALEIN TODAY

Kwajalein's fate is tied to the will and needs of the United States government and can change at any time. At the moment, the military leases seem likely to continue. Contractors will come out to work, mostly from the States, but some from other countries. Some stay for a few months, others for many years and enjoy a paradisiacal Pacific Island lifestyle. In some ways, the lives of the contractors are almost make-believe versions of island life, since they live without most of the hardships native islanders face daily. Like me, contractors enjoy beautiful white sand beaches, palm trees, and idyllic blue water. Locals often struggle just to get food and supplies.

Housing on the military base is built to standards that far exceed the living conditions of those living on nearby Ebeye or any of the other islands within the Marshall group. Contractors live in insulated houses and apartments with air conditioning, electricity, refrigeration, running water, and proper sewage disposal. These amenities are mostly lacking on Ebeye, which does have an electric generating plant, a water desalinization plant, and a sewage treatment plant (mostly built from foreign aid projects), but all three are in various stages of maintenance and decay. They work either sporadically or not at all.

The lives of U.S. personnel seem utopian compared with the way most Marshallese live. Just five miles north of Kwajalein Island, the island of Ebeye is one of the most densely populated strips of land on earth. Jobs provided by the Army base have attracted many to Ebeye from the outer Marshalls and from other parts of Micronesia. Other residents live off the paychecks of their families. Marshallese culture resembles many other Pacific Islander cultures, which make the highest priority taking care of one's immediate and extended family. It is a culture in which, if you need something and your neighbor has it, you have a right to borrow it, without asking, even if you don't give it back. The practice is not appreciated by the expats living on Kwajalein, who often find their bikes have been "borrowed."

While the U.S. military has created many jobs, it has also led to the overpopulation of Ebeye. And while employed Marshallese aim to better their lives, their cultural practices often hinder their doing so. Their goal may be to move to Hawaii for a better life, but wages spent on supporting an extended family of twenty souls typically makes that goal a forlorn hope.

On the man-made causeway connecting Ebeye to Guggegue Island

BATTLE SCARS

Occasionally, I got into discussions with my Marshallese ferry crew about World War II. They often repeated to me the stories their grandfathers and grandmothers had told them. When the Japanese took over Kwajalein prior to the outbreak of the war, they began building it up as a military base, forcing the Marshallese to serve as slave labor. Those who refused to work were killed. On these small islands with scant food and water resources, the Japanese made it illegal for the Marshallese to eat their own breadfruit, bananas, and even the fish they themselves caught. People were shot for picking the fruit from the trees that grew next to their houses. The trees and their fruit were the property of the Imperial Japanese Navy. Everything belonged to the Japanese.

The Japanese occupiers instilled in the Marshallese a fear of the Americans. "If you think we're bad," the message went, "just wait until you meet the Americans." But when the Americans won the islands—I was told—it was apparent that they were far more benevolent occupiers than the Japanese.

I hope the Marshallese still feel the same way, after the nuclear testing and the continual presence of the American military on Kwajalein. I've asked point blank, and they always said yes, the Americans provide jobs, so that people can support their families, buy things, and even possibly make their way to the United States. But the people of these islands are inclined to be courteous, and I am not certain they would have told me if they felt oppressed.

The Airplane Graveyard lies below the surface, mostly unseen and forgotten. We must not fail to see the people of the Marshall Islands, whose lives, like so many others around the world, are interwoven in our own and often governed by decisions made far away.

PBJ-1 Mitchell

Above: Ebeye child

Right: Kids playing on Ebeye

Left: Ebeye children make the most of anything they can find. Here they are playing in old refrigerators which float

Above: Ebeye girls peeking out from inside a house

ABOUT THE AUTHORS

BRANDI MUELLER is an award winning underwater photographer and writer who grew up in Northern Wisconsin. She considers herself an obsessive traveler and does everything she can to travel as much as often, mostly to scuba dive. She is also a 200ton USCG Merchant Mariner Captain and has been lucky to live and work in places such as Hawaii, the Marshall Islands, Micronesia, Papua New Guinea, Dominican Republic, Turks and Caicos, and more.

Brandi has published many articles and photos and is a regular contributor to Dive Photo Guide and X-Ray Magazine. Her work has also appeared in Scuba Diving Magazine, Asian Diver,Scuba Diver Australasia, Dive Advisor, in Lonely Planet books and magazines, newspapers and online on Mashable, MSN, Telegraph, The Blaze, Life Daily, AOL, Unilad, and ABC News, to name a few. She is an Ikelite Ambassador, a member of the Ocean Artists Society and has a bachelor's degree from the University of Tampa and a Master's degree from the University of Hawaii.

She is currently spending part of the year working in Chuuk, Micronesia, diving the WWII Wrecks of Truk Lagoon and the rest of the year traveling, often teaching underwater photography at festivals and workshops.

Brandi hopes her work will open up the underwater realm to the masses. The ocean is in trouble and there is a lot to preserve in the depths from World War II airplanes to fish, coral and other marine life. She hopes her images and words can help make a difference.

Propellers and SBD parts

ALAN AXELROD is the author of many books on leadership, history, and biography, including *The 30 Most Influential People of World War II* (Permuted Press), as well as *Lost Destiny: Joe Kennedy Jr. and the Doomed WWI Mission to Save London, Patton: A Biography, Bradley: A Biography, How America Won World War I, The Battle of Verdun,* and *The Battle of the Somme.* He was most recently a creative consultant and on-screen commentator for *The Great War,* on the PBS American Experience television series.

ACKNOWLEDGMENTS

When I reflect on everyone who helped me to this very moment, the linked list of people who influenced my diving and photography career goes on and on. My eternal thanks go to all of my diving instructors and the many people I have had the pleasure to work with and learn from, as well as the people who guided and supported me in my underwater photography endeavors. I may never have visited the Airplane Graveyard if my friends Amber Martin and Rob Clayton had not moved to Kwajalein, nor would I have had the opportunity to spend such a great deal of time diving them had Chugach Alaska Corporation not hired me to work on USAGKA. To everyone I've had the pleasure of diving with, specifically the members from Kwajalein and Roi-Namur Scuba Clubs, thank you for sharing the magic of being underwater with me.

Thank you to Michael Lewis and everyone at Permuted Press for presenting this opportunity and making it a reality. I am thankful for Alan Axelrod's contribution to the book. His eloquent writing and historical knowledge was imperative to its completion.

I am overwhelmed with gratitude to the brave WWII veterans; I cannot imagine their war-time experiences or what it must have been like for a few to watch their planes sink into the ocean. I wonder if it was a conclusion to their plight or if it was sad to watch them sink into the abyss. I can't help but also thank whoever made the decision to dump the planes inside the lagoon (100-120ft) and not on the Oceanside of the Atoll (1000+ft), so that today they are not too deep for recreational divers to visit. I'm glad these war birds have a chance to live on, even if it is underwater, providing a home for marine life and providing spectacular diving opportunities for those who find themselves on a tiny island in the middle of the Pacific Ocean.

Finally, I am entirely indebted to my amazing parents who have supported every "once in a lifetime" opportunity. Thank you for your endless support and encouragement.

—Brandi